World Governments

Authors: Daniel S. Campagna, Ph.D., and Ann B. Campagna
Editor: Mary Dieterich
Proofreader: Margaret Brown

COPYRIGHT © 2019 Mark Twain Media, Inc.

ISBN 978-1-62223-769-2

Printing No. CD-405035

Mark Twain Media, Inc., Publishers
Distributed by Carson-Dellosa Publishing LLC

Table of Contents

A Note to Instructors

The *World Governments* book explores how governments are formed, what institutions and processes are needed to sustain a government, and how governments around the world are similar and different. Topics covered include What Is a Nation?, key terms of world politics, types of world governments, the United Nations, international law, and the state of world governments.

World Governments compares 13 nations and governments from around the world. Each nation is profiled with information about the country, a brief summary of the type of government, and a discussion of current issues that are important to the nation. The reading selection is followed by review exercises that include matching, fill in the blank, and critical thinking exercises.

Internet links to more information about each country are provided in the reading selections and in the Reference Sources section at the back of the book. Students are encouraged to research each nation and type of government to enrich their knowledge of world governments and to complete extension activities.

Additional activities and challenges for student engagement are available at the back of the book.

- Challenge activity where students compare constitutions of various world governments

- Group exercise on developing a treaty among world governments

- Graphic organizer that allows students to compare and contrast countries and their governments

The goal of this book is to spark students' imaginations and develop an interest in countries around the world. By using the Internet, atlases, satellite imaging, and other resources, students can gain a wealth of knowledge about other nations and their governments. Hopefully, this will lead to a curiosity about the world, understanding of other cultures, and a desire to see these countries for themselves one day.

Section 1: Introduction

Welcome to *World Governments!* In this book, you will learn about nations and governments from all regions of the globe. There are about 195 independent states or nations in the world. Use this book to travel around the world and study different peoples, cultures, and the many ways that these countries function.

We will be discussing a variety of "hot button" topics such as:

- What is life like in a successfully governed nation?
- How does a nation fail?
- Where are people happiest (or not)?
- How has history shaped world politics?

There's much more to learn on this road to discovery. Our goal is simple—to introduce you to a mixture of 13 international governments. We will be your travel guides, so to speak, as we crisscross the globe. You will study 13 countries located in the six major geographic regions of the world. In Section 7: Asia, for instance, you will learn about the governments of China and Thailand. In Section 11: South America, we will look at how the nations of Brazil and Peru are governed. Each of the 13 countries represents one of the basic types of governments that will be talked about in Section 4: Types of World Governments and Political Systems.

Temple Wat Arun in Bangkok, Thailand

Also, you will have a chance to explore deeper into each nation's government, history, and culture. At the end of the book, there is a challenge activity where you can compare world governments and constitutions. A group activity also allows you to develop a treaty among countries.

Who knows? Maybe your imagination will be sparked by reading this book. You may decide to apply for a passport. A **passport** is a document, like a driver's license, that allows a citizen to travel to other countries. It is required for such travel. Without it, you may not be allowed to enter (or leave) another country. Every government in the world issues (makes) passports to its citizens. Think of it as an international I.D. card that verifies or proves you are a citizen of the United States.

In any event, we hope you will read this book with a sense of curiosity about the many types of world governments and cultures. With the Internet, e-mail, satellite imaging, cell phones, trans-global air travel, and a passport at your side (plus this book!), almost anyone can learn about world politics from the comfort of their homes.

Section 1: Introduction (cont.)

You will also be directed to specific websites. These sites will give you a chance to look at and read about current events in the 13 nations. We have handpicked these sites and believe there is something in them to interest most readers. For example, how would you like to take a look at a beautiful country full of exotic animals and plants? This country has no army, and its government is one of the most stable in Central America. Where is this nation? Welcome to Costa Rica.

Each of the 13 nations is organized in the following ways:

- **Name** of the nation

- **National motto**

- **Website** that directs you to information about that country and its government

- **Snapshot:** A few comments that provide a backdrop for understanding the country and its government

- **Government in a Nutshell:** A summary of the three branches of government: executive, legislative, and judicial

- **Major Issues:** serious problems and challenges that a nation is trying to overcome

- **What You Should Also Know:** bullet entries with quick facts about a nation and its people

Our advice is for you to take advantage of the materials in this book, ask about any topic that sparks your interest, visit the websites, have fun with the challenges, and see if you can answer the question "If you could travel anywhere in the world, where would you go?"

One last point. We assume that most of you have never traveled outside of the United States, that you do not own a passport, and that much of what you read and learn in this book will be new material. If you have traveled abroad—wonderful! Your experiences, your souvenirs or photographs, and your observations (French fries are served with mayonnaise in the Netherlands.) can be added to class discussions and projects. There's nothing like an "on the scene" reporter to help liven up a conversation.

Bon voyage! (Have a good trip!)

Section 2: Glossary—Key Terms of World Politics

Since it makes sense to understand what you are reading, we suggest you take a few minutes to look at (and remember) some of the following terms. You will see these terms in different sections. Learning what they mean will make your study of the world governments more useful. It will also help you connect ideas to actual events. In Section 6: Africa, for instance, you will discover that South Africa is a "developing nation." That means it has many of the things needed to move ahead with its economy, but there is much room for improvement. Once (and if) it solves problems such as poverty, crime, and the spread of AIDS, South Africa may move out of the realm of developing nation.

Practice saying the terms, and try giving a brief definition of them to others. After all, there are almost 200 nations in the world! That is plenty of governments and cultures to study. There are 13 nations in this book. Each has a different form of political culture and government. It is worth your while therefore to get used to these terms. Examine the terms below. Ask questions about any items that seem vague or hard to understand. And relax—once you master the terms, you'll have it! You will find that understanding ideas in this book will happen faster and easier as you move through the sections.

Terms

NOTE: e.g. is an abbreviation meaning "for example." This abbreviation is used throughout the book.

- **Capitalism** [**kap**-i-tl-iz-*uh*m]: Countries that allow capitalism encourage their citizens to set up and control businesses. The price of a product or service is based on consumer supply and demand (usually). For instance, if demand for oil drops, prices at the gas pump will also drop. Capitalism is based on the major idea of making profit through competition in an open market.

- **Colonialism** [k*uh*-**loh**-nee-*uh*-liz-*uh*m]: Simply stated, colonialism means a nation (usually a European country) explored and conquered another nation or country. Much of this activity happened between 1500 and 1950 in such places as Africa, North America, South America, Central America, Southeast Asia, and Australia. European nations used armed force, diseases, slavery, treaties, and settlers to take over other less-developed and weaker countries. They did this in order to gain natural resources, e.g., diamonds, gold, or fertile land, or for other military or political reasons.

Section 2: Glossary—Key Terms of World Politics (cont.)

- **Constitution** [kon-sti-**too**-sh*uh*n]: A list of values and basic ideas that state how a nation is to be put together and what rights citizens will have under that government. In the United States, the constitution lists a number of rights available to its citizens, e.g., the right to vote. These rights are found in the document known as the Constitution of the United States.

- **Developing Nation:** These are nations sometimes called third-world countries. The term refers to nations where major social problems occur often, like famine or starvation, diseases, and low incomes. Sometimes the governments of these nations are in flux—they change leaders often, the military gets involved, and the quality of life in general swings between bad and worse. An example of a result of living in a developing nation is short life spans for the citizens. That means disease, malnutrition (bad diet), pollution, wars, etc., reduce the chance of living a full life. Pakistan, Burundi, and Myanmar are examples of nations where the governments are very disorganized and corrupt.

- **Diplomacy** [dih-**ploh**-m*uh*-see]: This term has many definitions, but we will use a common one. Diplomary is the practice or art of settling problems between and among nations without using force. International law (see below) contains rules and agreements for nations to use in their negotiations. For instance, there are treaties or international agreements that ban slavery. In other words, nations talk about their problems rather than go to war with each other.

- **Economy** [ih-**kon**-*uh*-mee]: You hear about "the economy" daily in the news. Let us keep this one simple. The economy is all about the creation or production of goods and services. Goods are things made, e.g., computers, banjos, etc. Services are things done or processes, e.g., selling hamburgers, hiring a lawyer, going to the dentist. Put the two together —goods and services—and you have a rough idea of the gross (total) economic value of a nation.

- **Electorate** [ih-**lek**-ter-it]: People entitled to vote in an election because they have reached the age of suffrage. Suffrage means you are legally allowed to vote. In most countries, the age of suffrage or voting is 18.

- **Emerging Nation**: A nation that is slowly becoming developed. That means it has built industries like factories, power plants, and ports. An emerging nation usually is more successful; its people live longer, are better educated, eat better, and earn more money. They tend to be a happier electorate.

- **Exchange Rates**: This is a handy thing to know when you travel to another country. It is also a very accurate measure of a country's economic health. It refers to the comparison of a nation's currency (money) to that of another nation. For example, if the exchange rate is 42 Mauritius rupees (MUR) to one United States dollar (USD) it would look like this: 42 MUR = 1 USD. Every U.S. dollar would be worth 42 Mauritius rupees. That means the dollar is worth more (stronger in value) than the rupee.

Section 2: Glossary—Key Terms of World Politics (cont.)

- **Executive Branch** [ig-**zek**-y*uh*-tiv]: Think Prime Minister or President or Premier. This is the branch of government that attends to the daily operations of government, including such things as enforcing the laws of the country.

- **Globalization** [glow-b*uh*-l*uh*-**zay**-sh*uh*n]: There are lots of ways to define this term. The handiest is the idea of a world market. Through trade, migration or movement of people, and investments of money and industries across the world, globalization has changed how we view each other. A motorcycle, for instance, will probably have several parts made in different nations. The next time you go to the grocery store, read the labels carefully on the cans of food. Chances are the products were produced in one nation, packaged in another, and shipped or distributed from yet another nation. But here is the niftiest way to view globalization. With teacher supervision, go to the Internet site www.youtube.com. Type in a heading such as Egyptian rap music or Italian politicians. You will get immediate access to videos for both topics made in those countries. Those videos and the messages they contain are available to anyone in the world with an Internet connection. Welcome to globalization.

- **Government**: A government is the central group that uses its authority over the electorate (citizens). This also refers to the traditional branches of government known as the executive, legislative, and judicial. Most countries have these branches in some form.

- **Industrialization** [in-**duhs**-tree-*uh*-l*uh*-**zay**-sh*uh*n]: One of the necessary pieces of a successful and happy nation is money spent in manufacturing, technology, etc. Simply put, an industrialized country will be a modern one. The goods and services that we take for granted, such as computers, cars, movies, perfumes, the availability of fresh fruit year round, and drive-up banking, are examples of industrialization. That process, by the way, never ends. It requires a government and its people to constantly create new ideas and things.

- **Infrastructure** [**in**-fr*uh*-struhk-cher]: This is all of the internal items that are needed to keep a country running or functioning. It includes highways, the postal service, the water supply, power grids and plants, telecommunications (think cell phones), buildings, and so on. Without a well-run infrastructure, not much would get accomplished in a country. Developing nations rarely have a reliable infrastructure.

- **International Court of Justice**: This is the judicial arm of the United Nations. This court uses international law(s) to hand down decisions on conflicts between nations. The nations must agree to abide by the decision of the International Court of Justice. The court is located in the Peace Palace in The Hague, Netherlands.

Section 2: Glossary—Key Terms of World Politics (cont.)

- **International Law**: Just as each nation has its own set of laws to help govern itself, we need laws to help nations live together with each other. These laws are based on customs from the past, new agreements or treaties, and decisions issued by the International Court of Justice. If a nation wishes to claim the offshore fishing rights that rightfully belong to another nation, for instance, international law would apply.

- **Islamic Fundamentalism** [fuhn-d*uh*-**men**-tl-iz-*uh*m]: This is a movement that seeks to convert the world to the strict codes of behavior and laws of Islam. It dates back several hundred years. The movement does not recognize the need for equality of citizens, secular (nonreligious) government, religious tolerance, or the possibility that its basic beliefs are wrong.

- **Judicial Branch** [joo-**dish**-*uh*l]: The judiciary is one of the three traditional branches of government. A system of courts interprets and applies the law. That is how conflicts and disputes are settled.

- **Legislative Branch** [**lej**-is-ley-tiv]: The legislative branch makes, amends (changes), and repeals or throws out laws. Normally, the legislature can also impose or apply taxes and raise money for a state or country. Routinely, there is either one (unicameral) or two (bicameral) houses or chambers in a legislature.

- **National Defense**: Everything that a nation uses or produces to safeguard its survival, e.g., armed forces, political power, and economic force.

- **Political Parties**: A political party is a political organization that tries to get and keep political power within government, usually by backing candidates in elections. Each party has a viewpoint or ideology that represents the interests of the people and groups within the party.

- **Third World**: Countries in turmoil with marginal or weak economies. Third-world countries are weak in industrialization and infrastructure. Their governments are often corrupt or unstable, and the majority of people struggle to survive. This term is often used when referring to developing nations. Most of Africa, Central America, much of South America, and parts of Asia and the Middle East fall in the category of Third World.

- **United Nations**: A famous agency, the United Nations or UN is made up of 193 countries and was created in 1945 after World War II. The UN is based in New York City. Its primary goals are to protect global peace and solve major problems throughout the world. If a civil war breaks out in a third-world country, the UN may be asked to send in a military task force to keep the peace. There have been UN peacekeeping missions in the Western Sahara, Darfur, Timor-Leste, Cyprus, and Liberia, to name a few.

Name: _____   Date: _____

Section 2: Glossary—Key Terms of World Politics (cont.) Crossword Puzzle

Directions: Complete the crossword puzzle using the clues below.

ACROSS

2. everything that a nation uses or produces to safeguard its survival (two words)
6. branch of government that attends to the daily operations of government, such as enforcing laws
7. branch of government that makes, amends, and repeals laws
8. laws to help nations live together, based on customs, treaties, and court decisions (two words)
9. branch of government that is a system of courts that interpret and apply the law
12. an organization of 193 countries that tries to protect global peace and solve major problems around the world (two words)
14. a list of values and basic ideas that state how a nation is to be put together and what rights citizens will have under that government
16. a world market made possible by trade, migration, investment of money, and communication
17. the production of goods and services
18. the central group that uses its authority over the citizens of a nation

19. the never-ending process of being a modern nation through manufacturing, technology, etc.
20. nations talk about their problems rather than go to war with each other

DOWN

1. the movement that seeks to convert the world to the strict codes of behavior and laws of Islam (two words)
3. a nation that is slowly becoming developed (two words)
4. an organization with a certain viewpoint or ideology that tries to keep political power within government (two words)
5. sometimes called third-world countries; nations where major social problems occur (two words)
10. when a nation explores and conquers another nation or country
11. the voters
13. all of the internal items needed to keep a country running, such as highways, power plants, etc.
15. based on the idea of making profit through competition in an open market

Section 3: What Is a Nation?

The single most important idea in this book is **nation**. What makes a nation, and how does it function?

Let's start with the basics. A nation consists of the following elements or pieces:

- A **specific place** (geography) referred to as a country. This includes a clearly defined boundary.

- A **population or group(s) of people** who occupy the same place. This group may be broken down into various subgroups or ethnic groups, e.g., Indians, Taiwanese, and Bolivians. The United States, for instance, has many types of people from all over the world. They have one thing in common. The U.S.A. is the place they want to live.

- An **independent, central government** which is, hopefully, one that supports freedom and democratic values and promotes happiness. Normally, the government has a **tripodal** structure. This means the government has three parts, which are called the executive, legislative, and judicial branches. Please note that there are plenty of nations that do not have a tripod of branches or they are in a state of decline. The Republic of the Congo, Somalia, Haiti, and Chad are good examples of nations that have either no working government or are mired in civil wars and tribal conflicts.

- A **set of laws** to govern the people, such as a criminal code.

- **Recognized** by the rest of the world **as a sovereign (independent) nation** complete with its own flag, national anthem, and passport.

- Usually, but not always, a nation has **a common or shared language**. This means the language, e.g., English or Bantu, that most of the citizens speak in everyday use.

- **A working economy**. This means a nation is able to create income, mint money, and collect taxes. It also means that a nation has the ability to ship out (export) and bring in (import) products and services to/from other nations.

- **Basic care and services for citizens.** A true nation provides a level of basic care for its people in the form of schools, medical treatment, postal delivery, military defense, and so forth. These things are paid for by the economy. For instance, in Saudi Arabia many of these basic services are paid for by the revenue or income from the sale of petroleum (oil) to the rest of the world.

Section 3: What Is a Nation? (cont.)

- **Shared culture and values.** The people in a nation share many of the same basic beliefs and values (hopefully). In the United States, for instance, the majority of people support the principle of separation of church and state and the separation of powers in government. No matter where a person originally came from, e.g., Cambodia, Russia, or New Zealand, they become U.S. citizens and have one shared value—"We are all Americans."

- **A standard currency.** All nations need one common form of money, e.g., Indian rupees, British pounds, Japanese yen, etc., to carry out the day-to-day activities of business and spending.

- **National security.** All successful nations have some means or agencies (military) for keeping the peace. Defending oneself from aggressors is absolutely vital to a nation's welfare and independence.

- **Political system.** In addition to a basic government, a nation must include a system of ideals, processes, laws, and documents upon which a government is built. This means how things get done in the government. The nation of Jordan, for instance, has three branches of government. It has had a constitution since 1952. The political system includes Islamic laws and the legal codes of France.

There are many more items that could be added to this simple checklist. We could say, for example, that a nation includes a common system of education, an infrastructure (remember Section 2?), and so on. For now, however, this is a good starting point. There are nations, for example, such as Senegal and North Korea that satisfy most of the above items. However, they are not considered "healthy" places to reside. It is not enough, in other words, to identify the traits of a nation and assume all is well within it. Nor can we assume that a country that appears to have all of the pieces of a nation is what it seems to be. Haiti and Yemen, for example, are nations with "all of the political pieces," yet neither is stable, and neither is concerned about the safety and rights of its citizens.

As you will discover in the coming pages, a nation is more than a checklist of items. Now that you have a short introduction as to what the basic parts of a nation are, it is time to take a look at the various types of governments.

Section 4: Types of World Governments and Political Systems

In this book, we look at a number of governments and their **political systems** (how the government represents its people). One of the ingredients of a nation, you may recall from Section 3, is the presence of a functioning or working government. It may be a government and political system you do not like, such as a dictatorship or military junta (rule by force) or a system based on everyone receiving the same rights and benefits (socialism) through high taxes.

There are a handful of nations, however, such as Somalia, Cote d'Ivore, and Sudan, that are basically lawless. Government, rebel, and tribal forces are constantly fighting one another for control of the country. They do so in order to establish or create their version of a working government that a majority of the citizens will support. In those types of countries, power changes hands often. The government, or what is a shell of one, has little power to exert its will. A rival group may overthrow the government in what is known as a **coup** [koo].

So it does matter what type of government and political system you are reviewing. This is especially true if you ever plan on traveling to another country. Take a look at the entries below. Become familiar with some of the basic differences. The list of governments includes all of those mentioned in this book as well as some new ones. Combined, they represent the majority of the world's governments and political systems.

- **Constitutional democracy** <http://en.wikipedia.org/wiki/liberal_democracy>: This is a system of government derived from a constitution. That document is the basis for how the government will be designed and how it will function. Powers, rights, and authority (who gets to do what) are outlined in the constitution and the laws passed by the legislature. Its success and legitimacy (do people believe in it) requires mass support, known as a **consensus** or will of the people. This is a form of representative democracy. The people elect delegates to represent them in the government. Different forms of the constitutional democracy include the federal republic (United States, Brazil) and the constitutional monarchy (United Kingdom, Spain).

- **Communist state** <http://en.wikipedia.org/wiki/communist_state>: There are very few communist states or nations left in the world. In those nations, there is only one political party in charge. A central government sets policies, rules, and laws for all of the citizens. All branches of government are under the direction of a ruling body or council. Criticism and opposition to the government is not tolerated. Most of the country's wealth and power resides in the hands of those who run the Communist Party of that country. China, Laos, Cambodia, North Korea, and Cuba are examples of communist nations.

Section 4: Types of World Governments and Political Systems (cont.)

- **Constitutional monarchy** <http://en.wikipedia.org/wiki/constitutional_monarchy>: This is a government that has a **monarch** (king or queen) but one whose powers are limited by law or by a formal constitution. Examples of a consitutional monarchy are the United Kingdom, Jamaica, and Jordan.

- **Constitutional republic** <http://en.wikipedia.org/wiki/constitutional_republic>: This is government whose powers are limited by law or a formal constitution, and its leaders are elected. This is essentially a version of a republic. Peru is a constitutional republic (Section 11).

- **Democracy** <http://en.wikipedia.org/wiki/democracy>: A nation that claims to be democratic is one that supports the idea of majority rule. Such nations promote a wide range of liberties and freedoms, such as freedom of speech, assembly, and equal representation in government. To preserve that political system, it is vital to have free elections and a balanced government (all three branches).

- **Dictatorship** <http://en.wikipedia.org/wiki/dictatorship>: A nation with a **dictator** means one person has complete authority over a nation. Usually he acquires and keeps that position by force, threats, and punishment. Whatever political system is in place is secondary to the will and interests of the dictator. Individual rights are not important in a dictatorship. A dictator has absolute power over the electorate and typically relies on a loyal military to keep the government running. Another term for this type of quasi-government is **despotism**. Fortunately there are very few dictatorships left in the world. Burundi, North Korea, and Syria are examples of dictatorships.

- **Federal republic** <http://en.wikipedia.org/wiki/federation> or <http://en.wikipedia.org/wiki/federal_republic>: Put together a group of states or provinces within the same country, and you have what is known as a **federation**. The United States is a federal republic. Switzerland is also a good example of a federation. In that country, the **cantons** (or states) have certain rights and powers that cannot be altered by the central government. In return, the citizens of the Swiss cantons agree to support the central government in national matters such as national defense, education, and health 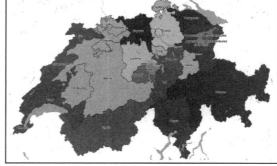 care reform. Power is shared, but ultimately, the central government must work with the cantons on behalf of citizens. This is very similar to the United States, where states have the authority to exercise power in some areas, but the final say in matters affecting the entire nation rests with the national government. Ethiopia, Indonesia, and Venezuela are also considered federal republics.

Section 4: Types of World Governments and Political Systems (cont.)

- **Islamic state** <http://en.wikipedia.org/wiki/Islamic_state>: There are governments, e.g., Saudi Arabia, Iran, and Syria, that emphasize the authority of the government based on the *Qur'an,* the basic text of Islam. Government heads or rulers are not elected. People are appointed to key posts in government, and elections often involve only one party or candidate. Citizens are granted a limited degree of freedom. The government is an extension of the state religion—Islam. Criticism of the government by citizens or the media is rarely tolerated and is often punished. The religion of Islam in those countries may never be challenged within the government. The *Qur'an* is the driving force behind the political process and system.

- **Monarchy** <http://en.wikipedia.org/wiki/monarchy>: A monarchy is a type of government (and the oldest one) in which one person inherits all political power. That power may be real or symbolic. England has a queen as a monarch, for instance, who has very limited actual power. Traditionally when a monarch dies, his or her **heir** (child or designated person) becomes the monarch. Nowadays, even though monarchs rule in various nations such as Brunei, Japan, Qatar, and Denmark, they are for the most part figureheads who lack any true political power.

- **Parliamentary democracy** <http://en.wikipedia.org/wiki/parliamentary_system>: This is a version of the constitutional monarchy. The members of the executive branch are chosen from the legislature (parliament). There is no clear separation of power. Both the executive and legislative branches must work together to draft and enact laws, set policies, and organize an effective government. Norway, Latvia, Great Britain, and Israel are examples of parliamentary democracies.

- **Republic:** <http://en.wikipedia.org/wiki/republic>A republic, like many of the types of government, comes in a wide range of flavors. In general, it is a government whereby the **electorate** (citizens who vote) keeps final control of the government in what is called the **rule of law**. Normally, it is the people who elect the lawmakers, executive, and judges for a central government. Having said that, however, it is worth noting that there are several types of republics, each one a bit different from the other! So, rather than confuse you with so many versions, let us stick with this generic description for the time being. South Africa is an example of a republic.

- **Political System:** <http://en.wikipedia.org/wiki/political_system> A political system is composed of the political parties and processes of a nation. Voting, for instance, is part of a process (how things are done) of a political system. This system helps keep the government functioning and the citizens happy (more or less).

Name: _____ Date: _____

Section 4: Types of World Governments and Political Systems (cont.) Word Search Puzzle

Directions: Find and circle the terms listed below in the word search puzzle. Words may be printed forward, backward, vertically, horizontally, or diagonally.

```
T L E W Y T W C K C L T N D L R L X B Q L N P
N C G T C D K R Z N R F L D M F F K E C D X A
V O N M A X E C U V N C N L K F T T V I P J R
J N T T R T C M Q L M H L X E W A X C T N K L
L S D D C B S R O R E M C D N T K T P J X Y I
T T M M O R T C Q C Z O E R S D A J Z H C H A
P I P F M W X M I R R F T B T L X B N R C M
J T R Y E F B B M M A A S L O J N Z T C M R E
C U Z R D R V N C T A I C R A H Z X I B R A N
K T R K L T K V I J N L S Y Y W K L R X G N T
R I N W A B L O Z U N H S T L D B Y M Z R O A
M O Z R N Z N X M T I W G I W U R Q L Z T M R
T N F P O W Y M Q P M M Z K P M W Y J X T L Y
D A L N I Y O X T T Z B L E B R N Y V M Z T D
C L T N T C N J V G G J R L Q K Y K B P K K E
G M J W U C P O L I T I C A L S Y S T E M K M
C O N S T I T U T I O N A L R E P U B L I C O
D N X L I N M T T H Q X N M M Z D T R V N T C
C A D K T F W L L W H Z J R P Y N Y V F K Z R
P R L R S X K G K K J T Q F L L T T R K M Y A
K C Q G N G R D E S P O T I S M N X H L P D C
K H M R O R C I L B U P E R L A R E D E F P Y
N Y M M C J K B B N T K B N X X G X Q X J Q B
```

COMMUNIST STATE
CONSTITUTIONAL DEMOCRACY
CONSTITUTIONAL MONARCHY
CONSTITUTIONAL REPUBLIC
DEMOCRACY
DESPOTISM
DICTATORSHIP
FEDERAL REPUBLIC

FEDERATION
ISLAMIC STATE
MONARCHY
PARLIAMENTARY DEMOCRACY
POLITICAL SYSTEM
REPUBLIC
RULE OF LAW

Section 5: United States of America

"In God We Trust"
<www.usa.gov>

Snapshot:

The United States of America is an excellent launch point for your study of world governments. In many ways, it is one of the easier nations to understand in terms of its government and political systems. About 326 million citizens live within its boundaries. These people represent every other country in the world. Every type of language, culture, customs, clothing, traditions—you name it—are all mixed in with one another throughout the 50 states.

We have fought two major wars on American soil, the War of Independence (also known as the American Revolution) against the British and the Civil War (the Union northern states versus the Confederate southern states). In both wars, one of the critical issues was how the country was to be governed and by whom. The War for Independence led to the construction of a Declaration of Independence, Constitution, and Bill of Rights that bound all states to uphold the central power of a newly formed **federal** or national government. The Civil War was a test of whether southern states should be **sovereign** (independent) of a federal government, especially in such areas as slavery and states' rights. If the Confederacy had won the Civil War, it is very probable that our country would have been divided into two distinct political systems and governments!

So, what concerns us in this section is how things turned out over the long run. In other words, what did our political structure become?

Government in a Nutshell:

The government of the United States is a **federal republic**. The people elect delegates to represent them in the government. This is a form of constitutional democracy, since the U.S. Constitution is the document that sets up how the government is organized.

For starters, think about the United States' political structure in terms of the "rule of three." There are:
1. Three tiers, or levels, of government: federal (national), state, and local (county and city), and
2. Each tier has three parts: executive, legislative, and judicial, and
3. Each of the three parts must work with each other in different ways to fulfill their duties.

Section 5: United States of America (cont.)

Keep in mind that the "glue" that binds all levels and parts of the government is the U.S. Constitution, the laws of the land, the federal system, popular support via elections, and a division of duties so each part knows what it is supposed to do. Without those pieces, not much would get accomplished. Let's take a closer look at the American system of government.

At the national level, popular support is shown by who we elect to represent us in the White House (president) and Congress (Senate and House of Representatives). The president, vice president, and his cabinet of advisors are the executive branch, or part, of the government. Congress is the legislative part. We do not elect federal judges. They are appointed by the president and approved by the Senate. All three units or branches must stay within their specific lines of authority. The president, for example, may not announce his own decision in a court case—that is beyond his authority. Nor could Congress sign its own treaty with another nation. The center of political power in the United States is Washington, D.C.

The **executive branch** of the government—the presidency—is also closely connected to international affairs. These duties include the following:

- Make treaties or agreements with other governments; this is done with the approval of the Senate
- Act as commander in chief of the armed forces (military)
- Appoint diplomats to represent the United States in other countries and at the United Nations
- Exercise discretionary emergency powers (declare martial law) in the case of a national disaster, e.g., terrorist attack

The two major political parties—Democrats and Republicans—control the Senate and

House of Representatives. It is a **bicameral** (two-house) legislature. The Senate has 100 members, two per state, who are elected to six-year terms. The House of Representatives contains 435 members who have two-year terms. The size of a state population determines how many representatives are elected to the House. Most of the time, **incumbents** (those people already holding office) get reelected. Oftentimes, the candidates spend millions of dollars to get reelected.

Section 5: United States of America (cont.)

In the **legislative branch**, Congress writes, reviews, and tries to approve the laws of the land. Congress has duties that often bring it into contact with foreign governments, such as working with diplomats and going to other countries on fact-finding trips. A few other important international powers include:

- Declaring war and approving peace agreements.
- Collecting taxes, borrowing, and making (minting) money.
- Regulating international trade agreements.

The **judicial branch** of government is represented by a federal, state, and local set of courts. Each set of courts deals with cases and issues tied to its jurisdiction. **Jurisdiction** means the authority of a court to hear and decide a case. A traffic court, for example, has no authority or jurisdiction to hear any cases not dealing with traffic matters. The highest court in the land is the **United States Supreme Court**. It is a court of appeals. That means a verdict or decision in a lower court may (not always) be heard in the Supreme Court. The judicial branch is independent of the other two parts of government.

Major Issues:

1. **Economy.** After years of slow recovery from the Great Recession of 2007–2009, by May 2018 the unemployment rate in the U.S. was at a new low and consumer confidence and spending was high. Increased business investing and tax cuts have led to more home building and higher wages. However, plans to increase tariffs on imports such as steel and aluminum from China and other trade partners have led to uncertainty about how this will affect the markets. If other countries raise tariffs on U.S. products, demand for manufactured and agricultural products could decrease. The challenge is to reach trade agreements with other countries that allow fair trade in both countries without engaging in a trade war where more tariffs are placed on each country's goods.

2. **Voter backlash.** It is fair to say that the political system of the United States has undergone major upheavals and conflicts. A loss of faith in government, especially in key areas such as the economy (see above) and two long, unpopular wars in Iraq and Afghanistan, have left the electorate (voters) unhappy and angry about "business as usual" in the national government. Historically, irate voters tend to create or move into splinter groups and try to make changes in the political arena. These groups usually are short-lived, have very narrow viewpoints, tend to rally around rabble rousers with little or no experience in government, and eventually fade from public view.

Section 5: United States of America (cont.)

3. **What to do with the neighbors!** The world has many dangerous places and people. At any given time, there are dozens of nations involved in civil wars or teetering on the brink of war. The U.S. and a global coalition of countries are involved in the civil war in Syria. They are trying to stop the spread of the Islamic State terrorist movement. Several other nations such as North Korea and Iran threaten to use nuclear weapons (weapons of mass destruction) against their enemies. Still

others, like Pakistan, Yemen, Somalia, and Indonesia, offer direct support and training to various terrorist groups. Add to this awful mix the prospect of famines, natural disasters (hurricanes, earthquakes), AIDS and other diseases, and renegade nations (Somalia and Sudan) all vying for our attention. The United States has devoted much of its resources to peacekeeping, sometimes to wars (Iraq and Afghanistan), and sometimes to relief efforts (Haiti).

What You Should Also Know:

- There are three major political groups or viewpoints in the United States: independent, conservative, and liberal. **Conservative** or pro-Republican regions of the nation are known as **red states**. More **liberal** or Democratic areas are called **blue states**.
- The United States is deeply tied to a military presence around the world. Military bases exist in about 800 sites, and troops are deployed in 150 other nations.
- The United States is a nation of urbanites; over 80% of the population live and work in urban (developed) regions of the country.

- The governments of the United States and Mexico continue to struggle with the crucial issues of illegal immigration, open trade, and drug trafficking.
- The national economy is the largest in the world. Translated: the financial health or woes of the United States are felt across the globe.

Name: _____ Date: _____

Section 5: United States of America (cont.)

Directions: Complete the following exercises.

Matching:

____ 1. bicameral

____ 2. federal

____ 3. incumbent

____ 4. jurisdiction

____ 5. sovereign

a. person already holding office

b. independent

c. two-house

d. national

e. authority of a court to hear and decide a case

Fill in the Blank:

6. The document that is part of the glue that binds all levels and parts of the U.S. government is the _____.

7. The three levels of government in the United States are _____, _____, and _____.

8. The three parts of each level are called the _____, _____, and _____ branches.

9. When voters get angry and form new groups to try to make changes in politics, it is called voter _____.

10. A case from a lower court may be appealed and heard again in the _____ _____.

Constructed Response:

11. Can the legislature pass whatever law it wants? How do the other branches of government keep it in check?

_____

_____

_____

_____

_____

_____

_____

Section 6: Africa—Republic of Mauritius [maw-**rish**-*uhs*]

"Star and Key of the Indian Ocean"
<www.govmu.org>

Snapshot:

This island nation is located several hundred miles off the east coast of Africa. It is one of the least known but more prosperous nations in the group of African nations. This is also remarkable since the island was empty of people until the 1600s. All types of people—Europeans, Africans, Indians— helped to settle/colonize the island. Ownership of the island has changed hands over the past three centuries, but on March 12, 1968, Mauritius was granted its independence from Great Britain.

Government in a Nutshell:

Mauritius is a **republic**. Every five years, the citizens gather to elect a new government. Like the United States of America, there are three branches of the government in Mauritius: executive, legislative, and judicial. Unlike most African countries, Mauritius is a peaceful, emerging nation. The goal of the government is to promote democratic values and ideals such as free speech, human rights, literacy, and a vigorous economy. The country is organized into ten districts (counties) and several small islands that depend on the government for support and services.

A president and a prime minister share **executive power**. It is easy to confuse the two offices, but keep in mind that the prime minister is basically the chief executive. The prime minister acts as a gatekeeper. He channels bills, advice, decisions, and so forth to the president for approval. A Council of Ministers (cabinet) help run the daily work of government and set the direction for new policies and programs. There are various ministries whose jobs are to carry out the decisions of the executive and legislative branches. Two examples of this would be a new program to increase voter turnout at elections or a decision to control water pollution.

The **legislature** is also known as the National Assembly or Parliament. It has 70 members. Three major political parties—Militant Socialist Movement, Social Alliance, and the Mauritian Militant Movement—represent the interests of the people. These parties, however, often add or shed other smaller political parties or interest groups. This is done in order to build a **consensus** (agreement) on some issue or bill. The National Assembly has only one branch or chamber (our U.S. Congress has the House of Representatives and Senate) to draft laws and represent all of its citizens. A member serves a five-year term in office.

Section 6: Africa—Republic of Mauritius (cont.)

Partly because of its small size and population, Mauritius has a small **judicial branch**. The key piece of the judicial branch is known as the Supreme Court. Six judges preside on this court. It has authority to oversee and hand down decisions over a wide range of legal matters. The laws of Mauritius reflect French and English legal influences or values. This is because Mauritius has a long history of involvement with these countries. At various times, the island was occupied by French or English troops.

Major Issues:

1. **Balancing act.** Mauritius struggles with the need for building up its economy while safeguarding the environment. Thus, water pollution, sewage, and garbage disposal remain problems for the government.

2. **Mauritius has no reservoir of natural resources** such as copper or oil. Its major resources are its people (about 1.2 million) and its land (sugar cane is its biggest crop). The island nation must find a way to grow without the benefits of a stockpile of natural resources.

What You Should Also Know:

- French and English are the most commonly spoken languages. This dates back to centuries ago when the French and English governments controlled the island at different times.

- Mauritius has no army. Like Costa Rica, it relies on police to enforce laws and provide national security.

- Trade, agriculture, some tourism, and manufacturing, such as clothing and electronic equipment, have helped make the island nation an economic success.

- Education is free for all citizens!

- There are no railroads, and huge traffic jams (gridlock) are very common in the capital city of Port-Louis.

- The government is focused on expanding the economy through competition and making the nation more modernized with better roads, more jobs, and more social services such as medical care.

- Mauritius is always warm, warmer, or very hot and humid. It is also a beautiful tropical nation with forests, beaches, and mountains.

- Keep up with the news of Mauritius by going to an excellent newspaper website: <http://www.allafrica.com>

Section 6: Africa—Republic of Mauritius (cont.)

Directions: Complete the following exercises.

Matching:

____ 1. National Assembly   a. minerals or substances from the earth like copper or
____ 2. republic   oil
____ 3. gridlock   b. agreement
____ 4. natural resources   c. a government elected by the citizens
____ 5. consensus   d. the legislature
                                 e. traffic jams

Fill in the Blank:

6. Mauritius tries to balance the need to build up its economy while safeguarding its
   _____.

7. The executive power is shared by a _____ and a _____
   _____.

8. The laws of Mauritius have _____ and _____ influences.

9. Mauritius has no army. The _____ enforce laws and provide national
   security.

10. Members of the National Assembly serve terms of _____ years.

Constructed Response:

11. What are some signs that Mauritius is a country that is on the right track?

_____
_____
_____
_____
_____
_____
_____
_____

Section 6: Africa—South Africa

"Unity Through Diversity"
<www.gov.za>

Snapshot:

As the name indicates, if you head to the southern-most part of the continent of Africa, you will find the nation of South Africa. It is about twice the size of Texas with a population of over 56 million people. It is not possible to understand the political system of South Africa without knowing a little something about its history.

South Africa was visited and settled by Europeans over 400 years ago, but native people have been living throughout South Africa for thousands of years. These various tribes came into armed conflict with French, British, Dutch, German, and Indian settlers and others who were intent on making their futures in South Africa. Each group brought with it a different set of laws and values. Each group treated the tribes as obstacles to their financial success. The different groups struggled and fought for hundreds of years but could not find a way to resolve their differences. In the end, the **immigrants** (white settlers) from Europe created and ran a working government even though they were a minority of the population. This changed in 1994 when Nelson Mandela, a black citizen, became President of South Africa. The system and practice of **apartheid** (racial segregation) slowly began to wither away.

Government in a Nutshell:

South Africa is a **parliamentary democracy**. If you refer back to Section 4, you will recall that a parliamentary democracy separates government power among three branches. These branches are called the executive, legislative, and judicial. It is designed to allow different groups of people representation in government. Since South Africa is a hodgepodge of tribes and ethnic groups from many parts of the world, representation of these interests is very important. Citizens with different viewpoints need to know that their beliefs are being heard in government. One unusual way that South Africa is different from other democracies is a matter of location. Each branch of government is located in a different city. Basically, there are three capitals!

The **executive branch** is situated in Pretoria. The president is the chief of state and head of the government and holds that office for a five-year term. The National Assembly (legislature) elects the president of South Africa. Some of the duties of the presidential office include:
- Chief of the military
- Appoints people to the Cabinet
- Speaks on behalf of South Africa to other nations
- Approval (or not) of bills and laws

Section 6: Africa—South Africa (cont.)

The **legislative** capital is found in Cape Town. The legislature or Parliament is split into two parts. The National Assembly has between 350 and 400 members who serve five-year terms. The National Assembly is like the U.S. House of Representatives. It is in the assembly that new laws are proposed and reviewed. The other half of the legislature is called the National Council of Provinces with less than 60 members. It is like the U.S. Senate and can propose certain types of laws. A helpful point of difference between the two is this—the bulk of the legislative work in South Africa happens in the National Assembly. And, the president picks his Cabinet from delegates in the National Assembly.

The **judicial** capital is the city of Bloemfontein. The court structure of South Africa is as follows:

- The highest court is the Constitutional Court. It only reviews cases that have some bearing or connection with the Constitution.
- The Supreme Court of Appeal is the court of final decision on all other types of cases that have no connection to a constitutional issue.
- The High Courts hear or review cases brought to them within a specific province. Circuit courts travel around the rural parts of provinces and hear cases.

From these three major cities the nine **provinces** (think states) of South Africa are governed. It is worth noting that the nine provinces of South Africa, like American states, have their own local governments. These local units clamor for more power and autonomy or freedom from the central government. Their citizens argue that they have a better idea of what their province needs to grow. The two largest provinces are KwaZulu-Natal and Gauteng with a combined population of over 20 million people.

Like the American system, South Africa has two major political parties. They are the Democratic Alliance Party (DAP) and the African National Congress or ANC. The ANC is the largest party. Other smaller parties exist such as the InKatha Freedom party, but by and large, much of the population belongs to the ANC or DAP. The African National Congress has played a very large part in the political process of South Africa.

Major Issues:

1. **Apartheid (see below) and the "brain drain."** There continues to be a migration or exit of highly educated and talented people from South Africa. They are in search of good-paying jobs and a stable future, neither of which are sure things in their native country.

2. **Rich man—poor man.** South Africa is reputed or known as a land of "uneven equality." Part of South Africa's success has been its transformation or change into a modern state. This includes lots of natural resources, ample highways, industries, tourism, and banking. However, there is still a nagging unevenness in people's incomes. This means many South Africans live in poverty (shanty towns) or work for marginal wages, barely enough to get by but never enough to get ahead. A small percentage of South Africans control much of the total wealth.

Section 6: Africa—South Africa (cont.)

What You Should Also Know:

- The past is never far behind the present in South Africa. As recently as the 1990s, the country was ruled by a minority of whites. This period is known as **apartheid**. Apartheid was racial segregation introduced through laws passed by a minority of whites who ran the government prior to 1994. It is worth noting that non-white people living with apartheid **could not do** the following:

Parliament Building

  1. They were unable to vote or hold public office.
  2. They needed a government pass to travel or work in much of South Africa. These passes were very rare.
  3. There were no civil rights of importance. Non-whites could be arrested and locked up indefinitely for no reason.
  4. There were very few services such as medical care, schools, and shopping for non-whites.
  5. There was complete separation of public facilities, e.g., white cinemas, black public restrooms, etc.

  This is a short list. It gives you a good idea of apartheid. Most of the South African population is black. With apartheid, most of the rights and privileges of government, like marriage, education, starting a business, etc., were not allowed for black people. Since 1994 (the end of official apartheid), the country has been trying to restore basic human rights to non-white citizens.

- The South African National Defense Force (SANDF) military is used to keep peace in many parts of Africa.
- This is a land of great appeal to tourists. Tourism is a major industry for the government. People come from all over the world to visit the game parks in South Africa. In these animal preserves, you can actually see and photograph lions, giraffes, rhinos, and hippos, who roam free in their natural habitats.

- There are actually **eleven official languages** recognized in South Africa! Many people speak more than one language.
- Because of the rapid spread of AIDS among the people of South Africa, it is estimated that over 3.7 million orphans (children without parents) reside in the nation.

Name: _____   Date: _____

Section 6: Africa—South Africa (cont.)

Directions: Complete the following exercises.

Matching:

____ 1. brain drain

____ 2. immigrants

____ 3. apartheid

____ 4. provinces

____ 5. parliamentary
democracy

a. states

b. racial segregation

c. government that separates power among three branches

d. highly educated and talented people leave

e. white settlers from Europe

Fill in the Blank:

6. Cape Town is the location of the _____ capital.

7. The white minority passed laws to keep the non-white majority segregated in a policy known as _____.

8. The judicial capital is the city of _____.

9. The president of South Africa is elected by the _____ _____.

10. The executive branch is located in _____.

Constructed Response:

11. What were some of the things non-whites could not do during apartheid?

_____

_____

_____

_____

_____

_____

_____

_____

_____

_____

Section 7: Asia—China

No official motto
<https://www.cia.gov/library/publications/resources/the-world-factbook/geos/ch.html>

Snapshot:

Explaining China and its political system is no easy task. China is the third-largest country in the world in area (Russia and Canada rank ahead of China) with a population close to 1.4 billion people! It shares borders with 14 other nations. China has only one time zone. It truly is a nation in which history has placed a heavy hand on the future. For over 3,500 years, China has had some form of government. The Mongol Horde, the Great Wall of China, centuries of dynastic and foreign wars, lots of inventions, Mao se Tung, and the rise of Communism are a few of the pieces of the large Chinese political puzzle. For example:

- China is the most populated nation in the world, yet it is governed in a way that is very odd. There are, in effect, two major political processes, one for the nation and one for the central government. Also, we do not truly know how some important decisions are made.
- China built one of history's first bureaucracies or set of government agencies to run the enormous country.
- It is a country with a written constitution that is not equally enforced or applied.
- China recently changed its "one child" policy to allow couples to have two children. The policy is meant to keep the population to a manageable size. Most Chinese prefer male children, as males are more valued in Chinese society than females.
- Luck and superstition play an important part in Chinese society. Red, for instance, is seen as a lucky color. People make all sorts of life-changing decisions based on lucky numbers, colors, compass points, etc.

There is much more that can be said about the mystery of China and its role in the world. What we need to consider, for now, is how the Chinese government is built to accommodate and absorb its past, its unique culture of luck, and the pressing need to run a massive country with almost 1.4 billion people. For that viewpoint we must look at the government and political system.

Government in a Nutshell:

China, also called the People's Republic of China, is a **communist state**, but it is in the midst of many changes to raise the standards of living for its people. These include such things as creating more jobs, exporting products, building power plants, adding more hospitals and schools, and competing in the global marketplace. So, we are faced with a situation that seems

Section 7: Asia—China (cont.)

to make no sense. With communism, a nation does not allow open competition of goods and services. The state or central government controls the means of production. Citizens are not encouraged to expect luxury items like cars, nice clothes, movies, and fancy haircuts. Yet many Chinese are able to purchase and enjoy these items. How does a political system claiming to be communist end up becoming so westernized? Let's begin with a look at the basic design of the Chinese political system. Bear in mind that this is not going to be a simple explanation. Chinese politics is something like a giant maze, after all, and getting a handle on it is no easy task!

There is only one political party—the Communist Party of China (CCP). Every eligible citizen belongs to it. To hold any national government office of real power one must be a member of the Communist Party. However, because China is so vast and heavily populated, it is necessary for the central or national government to delegate or allow many of its functions to be carried out by others in its 23 provinces (think states). These provinces are further broken down into prefectures, counties, townships, and even villages. Think of them as local units of government, much like counties, cities, and small towns in the United States. What binds all of these units together is the Communist Party and the central government.

A useful visual image of the Chinese political system is that of two intertwined ladders. Each ladder depends or leans on the other for support. The steps of the ladder represent the many types of government agencies and units that control and run the country. The Communist Party of China (86.2 million members), for example, is one ladder of the system. A small group of men are in charge of the Communist Party through the Politburo and its Standing Committee. A **politburo** is an executive group that makes most of the decisions for the political party, the CCP. They do so with the support of the army, called the PLA (People's Liberation Army). The Politburo decides priorities for the country. If, for instance, the Politburo thought it was in China's best future interests to explore outer space, it could recommend that money be spent for the building of a space station. On many other matters not directly tied to national well-being, however, decisions are often made by other groups. The Chinese Communist Party has committees throughout the country that can affect the decisions of local (provincial) governments. The CCP is very influential. Some young people join the party in order to improve their chances at better jobs.

The other ladder of the Chinese political system is more like the three tiers or levels of government found in most other nations. This is the national system of government with three basic arms or branches. The **executive branch** resides with the State Council. The

Section 7: Asia—China (cont.)

State Council is like a cabinet whose head is called the premier. The premier is the head of government. The president is the chief of state but has little actual power. He is a **figurehead** for the country (think monarch). The State Council group has its own standing committees and ministries to help it administer the country. A **ministry** is similar to a department in the United States. For instance, the United States Department of State has duties like those found in the Chinese Ministry of Foreign Affairs.

The **legislative branch** is composed of one chamber known as the National People's Congress (NPC). Its 3,000 deputies or representatives serve five-year terms and only meet for about two weeks a year. The NPC is supposed to make broad decisions for the nation and select its leadership, e.g., president, premier, etc. Critics claim that this legislature does not really have any authority. National elections for deputies, for example, are lopsided affairs. The ballot usually has only one candidate and that person is from the Communist Party. Also, the assumption or popular belief is that the more important decisions about government are made by officials outside the National People's Congress. Thus the "will of the people" is not accurately reflected in the legislature.

Too much resistance to the Communist Party or State Council by citizens or other groups normally leads to a crackdown on these persons by the People's Liberation Army (PLA). This makes the Chinese political puzzle even more curious. The military actually helps enforce the decisions of the Communist Party and the national government. Try thinking of it this way—imagine that the United States Congress passed a law that said the press could not criticize the government. To make sure the law was followed, the president ordered the National Guard in each state to supervise the press. While public opinion in the United States would not tolerate that action, it is allowed in China by the People's Liberation Army.

The **judicial branch** or court system is a bit less confusing. There are four levels to the Chinese court system:

1. Supreme People's Court; the highest court in the country. It can hear cases from any of the lower courts and make decisions on cases that are appealed.

2. Higher People's Court; these are found in the provinces. These courts review and decide cases or appeals that begin in or affect the province, such as a major crime.

3. Intermediate People's Court; such courts deal with legal matters in the capitals of the provinces and cases appealed to it from a lower court.

4. Basic People's Court; this is the bottom of the court system. These are local courts, sometimes made up of local people, who review criminal and civil cases within their township or district.

Section 7: Asia—China (cont.)

Keep in mind that all of these courts are supposed to decide their cases on the basis of what is in the best interests of the Communist Party. Any court that does not honor the basic ideals of Communism—the needs of the State are more important than those of any one person—may find its decisions or verdicts overturned by the Communist Party leadership or the PLA.

Major Issues:

1. **Local corruption.** A nation as big as China cannot supervise or watch over all of its officials. The further away a province is from the capital of Beijing, the more likely it is to encourage the abuse of power by its local political officials. In some places, laws do not get enforced or people are mistreated by their local government leaders.

2. **Pollution.** China is a nation undergoing vast upgrades. Power plants, new industries, and natural resources are being developed. However, the result is widespread unregulated air, water, and soil pollution. In some areas, the rivers have enough chemicals dumped into them to turn their color from brown to yellow, red, or green. Some major cities are beset or stuck with regular clouds of orange, gray, or yellow pollution. In fact, the most polluted cities in the world are located in China.

3. **Human rights violations.** The Communist Party and national government of China do not tolerate **dissent** or disagreement by its citizens. China has often been accused of denying basic rights and freedoms, such as freedom of speech, to its citizens. Critics also claim that the government has used illegal methods, e.g., torture, to control its people.

What You Should Also Know:

- All men between the ages of 18 and 22 must serve in the armed forces. Women are not exempt. They must also serve in assigned military jobs.

- China continues to open its trade and businesses to the outside world and has achieved great success in developing its economy. It is now the second largest economy in the world, behind the United States.

- Because of its thriving economy and a large military, China is seen as one of the most powerful nations in the world.

Name: _____ Date: _____

Section 7: Asia—China (cont.)

Directions: Complete the following exercises.

Matching:

____ 1. politburo

____ 2. ministry

____ 3. figurehead

____ 4. dissent

____ 5. corruption

a. similar to a department in the executive branch

b. disagreement

c. when officials abuse their power

d. chief of state with little actual power

e. executive group that makes most of the decisions for the only political party

Fill in the Blank:

6. Usually with _____, the central government does not allow open competition and controls the means of production.

7. However, China is trying to raise the standards of living for its people, so it is creating more _____, exporting products, and _____ in the global marketplace.

8. The only political party is called the _____ _____ of _____.

9. The politburo makes most of the decisions for the party with support from the _____ _____ Army.

10. Deputies for the National People's _____ only meet for about two weeks a year.

Critical Thinking:

11. If China does not give its citizens basic human rights, can it be considered a successful nation? Give specific examples to support your answer.

_____

_____

_____

_____

_____

Section 7: Asia—Thailand [TYE-land]

"Unity amongst those uniting brings about success and prosperity"
<https://www.cia.gov/library/publications/resources/the-world-factbook/geos/th.html>

Snapshot:

Thailand was once known as Siam. It is a completely independent nation. That is to say, Thailand has never been conquered and settled by other nations. It has had its share of invaders through the centuries, but none have been able to assume control of the country. The Thai people are proud of their heritage of freedom. Through the centuries, a series of kings or monarchs have tried to rule the country, some more successfully than others. Thailand has undergone a variety of governmental

forms—dictatorships, military takeovers, pure monarchies—over the years. Since 1932, the constitution has been changed 20 times! Today Thailand is mostly a **constitutional monarchy**. We say mostly because, from time to time, the country is faced with political strife from outside groups, e.g., military, who think the government is wrong or corrupt.

Government in a Nutshell:

The government of Thailand has a hereditary king as the chief of state. This means someone is monarch because they inherited the job from their ancestors and family. It does not mean the monarch is able or talented but simply that the person was born into the job. In Thailand, the king is a figurehead. He is expected to be a symbol of justice, strength, and virtue (good behavior) for the people of Thailand.

The **executive branch** of government is led by a prime minister. He is elected by the lower house of the legislature and appointed by the king. The prime minister chooses who will serve as his advisors on the cabinet. These various deputy ministers attend to a wide variety of matters such as energy, agriculture (farming), and science for the nation's 76 provinces (think counties). In the end, the prime minister is held accountable for the success or failure of the government. It is this person who represents the interests of Thailand at home and overseas. Also, the prime minister can be removed. This is a process that occurs within the legislature (House of Representatives). The members of the legislature, after much debate, may decide that a vote is needed. The vote is one of "confidence" (keep the prime minister in office) or "no confidence," which leads to the ouster or removal of the prime minister. A ready example of the process in action is the controversy surrounding the office of prime minister since 2008. Several would-be prime ministers have come and gone between 2008 and the present. Some were removed by the Constitutional Court, another was given a vote of no confidence, and yet another resigned! The current interim prime minister is a general appointed after he staged a takeover from the previous prime minister.

Section 7: Asia—Thailand (cont.)

The government in Thailand is in transition after a coup in 2014. The **legislative branch** is called the parliament or National Legislative Assembly. It is a two-chamber or **bicameral** body. Elections are scheduled for November 2018. The upper house or Senate will have 250 members appointed by the military for five-year terms. The Senate has certain exclusive powers. These are things that only the Senate is allowed to do, such as:

- Create committees to study matters or issues affecting the nation.
- Consider bills approved by the House of Representives.
- Decide how it will operate the Senate (rules and regulations).

The second chamber of the parliament is the House of Representatives. The 500 members will be elected for four-year terms. It is in the house that much of the real legislative activity takes place. The house, for instance, has the exclusive power to:

- Draft and prepare bills to be made into law.
- Remove the prime minister with a vote of no confidence.
- Order the members of the cabinet to appear and answer questions about their actions and decisions.

The house has several political parties such as the Thai National Development Party, For Thais Party, Democrat Party, and the Proud Thais Party. Ninety-eight new political parties had registered by April 2018. Each has its own platform or list of issues and values to promote, including economic growth and better health care.

There are three separate systems in the **judicial branch** of the Thai government:

1. Court of Justice; primary courts of the land. These courts hear criminal and civil cases.

2. Administrative Court; These courts settle complaints between citizens and the government.

3. Constitutional Court; Anything dealing with the constitution is decided in this court, e.g., removal of the prime minister.

Unfortunately the legal system of Thailand has a bad reputation for being corrupt, confusing, unfair, and using overly harsh penalties. Written records are not kept in the courts of justice. Juries are not used in trials. Confessions are sometimes forced from a defendant through torture and threats. Cases can be dragged out for years. Critics claim that the legal system of Thailand has been "adjusted" to meet the needs of those in power, including the military and the executive branch.

Section 7: Asia—Thailand (cont.)

Major Issues:

1. **Political stability.** Thailand has undergone various shifts in its political system for many years. It was not until 2001 that the government of Thailand was able to complete its first full term without disruption or removal. In 2006, the military overthrew the government. A few years later, the military leaders were partially ousted from their positions in government. Another coup took place in 2014. A general is now the interim prime minister. New elections are supposed to take place in November 2018. As you can see, the nation is still wrestling with the basic problems of managing unrest and public dissent without using force or corruption.

2. **Trafficking (dealing) in the purchase and sale of drugs and human beings.** Thailand has struggled with its global image of being a transit point for drug distribution and consumption. Neighboring countries of Laos and Myanmar use Thailand as a handy shipping point for drugs and as a destination for widespread sale of addictive drugs. People are also bought and sold in Thailand as servants, slaves, and unpaid laborers or workers.

What You Should Also Know:

- Thailand is an industrialized nation, but it is also a major exporter of rice.

- Most of the population belongs to the Buddhist religion.

- Criticizing the king is against the law.

- Thai boxing or *Muay* is taught at Buddhist temples to pupils.

- Education is free through grade 12.

The Temple of Dawn in Bangkok, Thailand

Section 7: Asia—Thailand (cont.)

Directions: Complete the following exercises.

Matching:

____ 1. vote of confidence

____ 2. constitutional monarchy

____ 3. bicameral

____ 4. agriculture

____ 5. trafficking

a. farming

b. dealing

c. government with a king or queen whose powers are limited by a formal constitution

d. a vote that keeps the prime minister in office

e. two-house

Fill in the Blank:

6. In Thailand, the king is a _____ who is expected to be a symbol of justice, strength, and virtue.

7. The legislature may remove the prime minister from office with a vote of _____ _____.

8. The Thai House of Representatives has the power to draft and prepare _____ to be made into law.

9. _____ are not used in trials in Thailand.

10. Addictive drugs from _____ and _____ are shipped through and sold in Thailand.

Constructed Response:

11. The government in Thailand has undergone many changes in its history. Give at least three examples of political instability in Thailand.

_____

_____

_____

_____

_____

_____

_____

Section 8: Central America and Caribbean Basin— Costa Rica

"Long live work and peace"
<https://www.cia.gov/library/publications/resources/the-world-factbook/geos/cs.html>

Snapshot:

Costa Rica is one of the more appealing nations in the world. The common language is Spanish. Its boundaries or borders are with Nicaragua (north), Panama (south and east), and two bodies of water—the North Pacific Ocean (west) and the Caribbean Sea (east). This is a country where history has played a big part in the shaping of Costa Rica's government and culture. Until the Spanish **conquistadores**, or soldiers of fortune, arrived in the 1500s, the country was fairly stable. The Spanish, including Christopher Columbus, brought diseases, infections, slavery, and brute force to the country and its native people. The result was that most of the native people died or fled from the Spanish. Most Costa Ricans today are of European descent. They brought with them many of the ideas and laws of their native countries that led to the creation of a Costa Rican government.

Government in A Nutshell:

This is a pretty straightforward, easy-to-understand political system. Costa Rica is a **democratic republic**. It has a constitution that endorses a system of checks and balances, much like that of the United States. The nation uses a system of checks and balances in which no single branch of government is the most powerful. There are three branches of government: executive (president), legislative (law-making), and judicial (a Supreme Court). Unlike the **executive** branch in the United States, there are two vice presidents. A person can only serve one term as president. He or she must then wait eight years before running for reelection. In 2010, Laura Chinchilla became the first female president of Costa Rica. The president can choose anyone to serve on the cabinet of advisors without needing a review from the legislature.

In the **legislature**, known as the Legislative Assembly, 57 representatives or delegates are elected to four-year terms of office. They cannot repeat their terms until they have sat out or not run for the office for four years. This gives more citizens the chance to serve in the national legislature. Ideally, no one clique or group of people can control the legislature for decades. The national budget is drafted and passed by the legislature. There are over a dozen political parties, such as the Social Christian Unity Party (PSUC), the National Liberation Party (PLN), and the Citizen Action Party (PAC).

The **judicial** system or Supreme Court has four units. Each deals with a general area of the law, such as the constitution and criminal law. It enjoys a great deal of freedom to

Section 8: Central America and Caribbean Basin— Costa Rica (cont.)

interpret the laws of the legislature and review cases and the decisions of the rest of the government. There are 22 judges who serve in the judiciary. Each has an eight-year term of office. The Legislative Assembly, not the citizens, elects these judges through a direct vote of the delegates.

In addition to the three branches of government, Costa Rica has several other political offices. These offices help run the country (the capital is in San José) and its seven major provinces. They include the Supreme Electoral Body, the Office of the Comptroller General, and others. It was only in the last decade that Costa Rica allowed for the election of mayors for the provinces. The government, with its rotating members of the legislature, changing presidents, and special units, is able to administer the entire nation of 4.3 million people.

Major Issues:

1. **Immigrants.** Illegal immigrants (refugees and workers) from Nicaragua and other countries in Central America pose a serious threat to the social welfare system of Costa Rica. This means that poverty affects about 20% of the people. Social services, like medical care and schooling, cannot keep pace with the volume of immigrants working in the country.

2. **Inside/outside.** Looking in from the outside, Costa Rica is an incredibly beautiful country with volcanoes, rain forests, beaches, mountain peaks, and a lush green umbrella of cloud forests. However, once you get inside, you see the problems of pollution, sanitation, and a "beat-up" infrastructure. The network of roads needs repair. A modern sewer and waste  treatment system is lacking. While this natural paradise appears unmarked by the effects of industrialization and the pressures of a growing population, the truth is that Costa Rica strives hard to match the outside appearance with its "inside" look. The government has put into place many reforms and laws meant to protect the natural beauty of the country.

What You Should Also Know:

- Costa Rica has no army. The country has been at peace for almost 60 years. It has dedicated itself to social reform and the protection of its environment.

- It is the most stable and democratic nation in Central America.

- Tourism is a huge source of foreign exchange (money from tourists) as people from other countries come to inspect the ecosystem (and try the surfing!).

- Most citizens in Costa Rica are educated (close to 100%). Schooling is mandatory.

Name: _____ Date: _____

Section 8: Central America and Caribbean Basin—Costa Rica (cont.)

Directions: Complete the following exercises.

Matching:

_____ 1. illegal immigrants

_____ 2. Legislative Assembly

_____ 3. democratic republic

_____ 4. conquistadores

_____ 5. foreign exchange

a. the legislature of Costa Rica

b. Spanish soldiers of fortune

c. money from tourists

d. refugees and workers who enter the country without proper paperwork

e. government where the people elect officials and the constitution sets up checks and balances

Fill in the Blank:

6. Costa Rica is the most stable and democratic nation in _____ _____.

7. _____ is the common language of Costa Rica.

8. The executive branch of government has two _____ _____.

9. Delegates to the Legislative Assembly cannot repeat their _____ until they have sat out for four years.

10. While Costa Rica has a beautiful ecosystem, the _____, such as roads and sewers, needs to be repaired and replaced.

Constructed Response:

11. Why are illegal immigrants a problem for the government of Costa Rica? Give specific examples to support your answer.

_____

_____

_____

_____

_____

_____

Section 8: Central America and Caribbean Basin— Honduras

"Free, Sovereign, and Independent"
<https://www.cia.gov/library/publications/resources/the-world-factbook/geos/ho.html>

Snapshot:

Honduras is one of the poorest, most unsettled countries in Latin America. Think of it as a complete opposite to Costa Rica. It has an estimated population of around nine million people. As you will soon discover, there is very little about Honduras that lives up to its national motto (see above). By the time Christopher Columbus arrived in 1502, the once mighty Mayan culture and people in Honduras had disappeared. Honduras became part of the Spanish empire in Latin America for several centuries. It gained its independence in 1821.

Honduras has been plagued by a series of upheavals, both man-made and natural. Governments have come and gone in a series of seesaw elections. Even worse, the country has been devastated by disasters. In 1998, Hurricane Mitch wiped out most of the highways, communication networks, and 70% of the crops. Thousands of people were killed or injured and over 80,000 homes damaged or destroyed. In 2008, floods washed away at least half of the roads.

Government in a Nutshell:

While the country of Honduras has undergone many hardships, its government is usually in a state of flux (change). Honduras often claims to be a **democratic constitutional republic**, but this is not always the case. Honduras does have the three branches of government, but they function based on the whims of whoever is in power. In 2009, the army expelled the previous president. A conservative candidate was elected and took office in January 2010. Juan Orlando Hernandez Alvarado has been president since 2014. The **executive** head or president serves a four-year term and shares some of his authority with the legislature. The Honduran constitution does give the president a wide range of powers including:
- The authority to represent Honduras in many matters
- The power to declare war and act as commander in chief of the military
- The power to manage the national treasury
- The right to veto or block laws passed by the legislature

The **legislative** branch is called the National Congress. It is **unicameral** (one house) with 128 members who serve four-year terms. These members are elected from the 18 departments of Honduras. A **department** is similar to a county or province. There are two major political

Section 8: Central America and Caribbean Basin— Honduras (cont.)

parties—the Liberal Party and the National Party. A few smaller parties exist, but most of the 128 members in the National Congress are aligned with either the Liberal or National Party.

The **judicial** branch is independent of the other two arms of government. It is made up of 15 judges who serve seven-year terms in the Supreme Court of Justice. Sometimes the Supreme Court uses its position to order other branches of government, such as the military, to take action. For example, Honduran law forbids citizens from being expelled, yet President Zelaya was expelled. Honduran law, mostly Spanish in its origins, forbids the denial of basic human rights, yet Honduran police and military routinely arrest and lock up citizens without a warrant or benefit of a hearing.

Major Issues:

1. **Gangs.** One of the man-made disasters facing Honduras is the growth of street gangs. Two of the more dangerous gangs are the 18th Street and MS-13 gangs. These gangs sell and distribute drugs, kill people, and try to undermine the government. These gangs make the country unsafe for many people.

2. **Immigration.** Poverty makes people move toward the promise of hope somewhere else. In Honduras, a small number of people own and control most of the wealth. The result is a very large portion of the electorate is poor with no real hope for improvement in their native country. Thus, Hondurans migrate to the United States and other Latin American countries, e.g., Costa Rica, in search of jobs, medical care, and schooling.

3. **A poor nation.** Honduras is very poor, badly managed, kept going through military force, and seen as a "sinking nation" rather than a democratic constitutional republic. It relies heavily on foreign aid from the United States to pay its bills. Many government projects, such as bridge building and proper sanitation, are not completed because the government runs out of money.

What You Should Also Know:

- Less than half of the children of Honduras complete elementary school.

- Soccer (football) is the national sport.

- Honduras has a huge variety of plant types or species (6,000), reptiles, birds, and mammals.

- The rate of unemployment hovers between 5% and 7%, and many people who have jobs are still unable to support themselves and their families.

Section 8: Central America and Caribbean Basin—Honduras (cont.)

Directions: Complete the following exercises.

Matching:

____ 1. democratic constitutional
         republic

____ 2. flux

____ 3. executive

____ 4. department

____ 5. unicameral

a. president

b. government where the people elect officials and the
   constitution sets up checks and balances

c. one-house

d. change

e. similar to a county or province

Fill in the Blank:

6. The three branches of government in Honduras function based on the _____
   of whoever is in power.

7. The _____ has the power to veto laws passed by the legislature.

8. By the time Christopher Columbus arrived in Honduras, the once mighty _____
   culture and its people had disappeared.

9. Natural disasters have devasted Honduras. _____ _____
   wiped out most of the highways, communication networks, and 70% of the crops.

10. Street _____ sell and distribute drugs, kill people, and try to undermine the
    government.

Constructed Response:

11. Why is Honduras seen as a sinking nation? Give specific examples to support your
    answer.

    _____

    _____

    _____

    _____

    _____

    _____

Section 9: Europe—Switzerland

"One for all, all for one"
<https://www.cia.gov/library/publications/resources/the-world-factbook/geos/sz.html>

Snapshot:

Switzerland is a special country that shares borders with five other western European nations. To get some sense of what makes Switzerland unique, keep the following facts in mind:

- It is one of the richest countries in the world.
- The quality of living (long lives, good health, happy people, etc.) is among the highest in the world.
- Even though the famous Swiss Alps and Jura Mountains cover 60% of the land, the population of Switzerland is about 8.2 million.
- Neutrality: Switzerland has remained neutral (stayed out of wars) in all major conflicts of the 20th and 21st centuries.
- Switzerland is seen as one of the most prosperous, stable, and "livable" nations in western Europe.

The country has been heavily influenced by the cultures and values of its neighbors. There are, for example, four official languages: French, Italian, German, and Romansch. In addition, many cultural items such as foods, clothing, business habits, and social values have been absorbed by Switzerland's closeness or proximity to its neighbors. The citizens place a high value on their nation's independent approach and role in foreign affairs.

Government in a Nutshell:

Switzerland is a **confederation** or union of **cantons** (states) with a federal constitution dating back to 1848. The cantons are very independent with plenty of authority. There is a central government that oversees matters affecting the entire nation. Much of the daily work of government, however, occurs within the cantons. This is an expression of the Swiss desire for freedom and neutrality. Each canton is, so to speak, its own government. There are 26 cantons. Even with the dispersal of power across the country, it is also true that the Swiss government and society are devoted to capitalism and the creation of wealth. Like Singapore and Hong Kong, Switzerland is known for its focus on trading, industry, and banking.

The **executive** branch is also different from many other countries. The Swiss Parliament or Federal Assembly elects seven citizens to serve on the Federal Council. Each member has a four-year term. Every year, a new president is elected from the Council by the Parliament to serve as the head of the federal government. The president of Switzerland, therefore, has no special powers or authority. For instance, the president cannot veto or stop a law. The president

Section 9: Europe—Switzerland (cont.)

is part of the Federal Council and helps run the country. The parliament has traditionally been the most powerful branch of government. This reflects a belief by the Swiss that the will of the people is a true measure of authority. Thus the cantons remain independent "kingdoms" of sorts who work together on national issues like air pollution, crime, and health care. The presidency is not meant to be a career position for any citizen.

The **legislative** branch is the source of much power in Switzerland. Called the Federal Assembly or parliament, it has two chambers (bicameral): the Council of States (46 representatives) and the National Council (200 members). Members of the Federal Assembly come from one of the many political parties in Switzerland. However, only four major parties have wielded power in the Swiss political process: the Swiss People's Party, the Christian Democrats, the

Swiss Bundeshaus (Parliament Building)

Liberal Democrats, and the Social Democrats. As noted above, the parliament decides who gets to be president, what laws are passed (or not), and can override some decisions of the executive branch. Interestingly enough, the Federal Assembly can be challenged by the electorate or voters. If a group is unhappy with a law and can collect 50,000 signatures within 100 days of the law's enactment (passage), a national vote is held. This is referred to as a **federal referendum**. It gives the average citizen a means to test the popularity of a law through an election.

The **judicial** branch is relatively simple. It consists of a federal supreme court with judges elected by the parliament for six-year terms of office. Other courts of the federal judiciary include the criminal court and administrative court. Much of the judicial work in Switzerland happens in the cantons, not at the federal level. Federal courts, by and large, tend to hear civil and criminal cases brought to them on appeal.

It is evident that Switzerland's political system is based on the principle of individual rights protected by the cantons. The cantons have their own governments, laws, constitutions, forms of administration or "ways of getting things done," and sets of group values and norms. The cantons have ample freedom to choose their own paths in most domestic matters, e.g., welfare services, licensing, etc., but they defer to the federal government in matters that affect most or all of the cantons, such as homeland security.

Section 9: Europe—Switzerland (cont.)

Major Issues:

1. **Dirty money.** Switzerland continues to hold the title of money-laundering capital of the world. Drug traffickers and other criminals are still able to place their illegal wealth in banks with little or no scrutiny or attention from the Swiss government. In recent years, it has worked to reform its banking secrecy laws.

2. **Rural flight.** At least two-thirds of the population of 8.2 million people in Switzerland have moved into urban areas to such big cities as Zurich, Lausanne, and Bern. This has put a growing strain on city resources such as electric power, recycling efforts/landfills, and police services (more crime).

What You Should Also Know:

- Any citizen 18 years or older can run for any office.

- All male citizens must serve in the Swiss Armed Forces at age 19. Women may voluntarily serve in the Armed Forces. Soldiers are required to keep all of their military equipment, e.g., uniforms, weapons, etc., at home.

- Switzerland's primary export is chemicals (but do not forget the chocolate and watches). It depends on its exports for economic growth.

- Health insurance is mandatory, and health care is seen as some of the best in western Europe.

- Switzerland has very few natural resources.

Name: _____ Date: _____

Section 9: Europe—Switzerland (cont.)

Directions: Complete the following exercises.

Matching:

____ 1. Federal Council

____ 2. canton

____ 3. federal referendum

____ 4. confederation

____ 5. neutral

a. a union of states with a federal constitution

b. seven citizens elected to help run the country, one of whom is elected to be the president

c. state

d. stays out of wars

e. a national vote on a law

Fill in the Blank:

6. Switzerland is known for its focus on trading, industry, and _____.

7. _____ _____ is a problem because two-thirds of the population has moved into urban areas.

8. The _____ has traditionally been the most powerful branch of government.

9. Criminals are able to place their illegal _____ in Swiss banks with little or no attention from the government.

10. Much of the daily work of government is done within the _____.

Critical Thinking:

11. Do you think it is a good idea for the parliament to have so much power? Give specific examples to support your answer.

_____

_____

_____

_____

_____

_____

_____

_____

Section 9: Europe—Spain

"Further Beyond"
<https://www.cia.gov/library/publications/resources/the-world-factbook/geos/sp.html>

Snapshot:

Spain is a very interesting country. Find it on a map. You will see that its location on the western edge of the Mediterranean explains some of its history. At different stages in history, Spain was occupied or controlled by the Roman Empire, Muslims from North Africa, and France. The country has been involved in many wars in the last several centuries. The most recent internal war—the Spanish Civil War (1936–1939)—resulted in a system of government known as fascism. General Francisco Franco became the dictator of Spain. Franco controlled every branch of government and used secret police and military to keep the citizens in fear. With **fascism**, independent rights are second to the will of the dictator (much like North Korea and Myanmar). When Franco died in 1975, things changed for the better in Spain. Juan Carlos became the King of Spain. A formal, written constitution was approved based on the ideals of democracy, such as freedom of speech, open elections, and so on. King Felipe VI has been king since 2014.

Government in a Nutshell:

Spain is viewed as a **parliamentary monarchy**. It has a king, a president, a legislative and judicial branch, and a Council of Ministers (cabinet). The government is based on a constitution that outlines the duties and powers of all branches and units. Thus far, the political system of Spain seems very simple and straightforward. It resembles other countries such as England and Thailand in the way the governments are run. But Spain is different in several important ways, as you shall see.

The **executive** branch consists of a **hereditary** (by birth) monarch and a president who selects a Council of Ministers. The king nominates someone to be the president. That person must be approved by the lower house of the legislative branch called the Congress of Deputies. The president is chosen from the political party in the legislature that has a **plurality** (most votes). So, unlike the United States, for instance, the president of Spain is not directly elected by the voters. Along with the Council of Ministers and Council of State, the president is expected to help run the national government.

The **legislature** is known as Las Cortes Generales or the National Assembly. It is **bicameral** (two chambers or houses). The houses are called the Congress of Deputies and the Senate. Both groups serve four-year terms of office that run concurrently (at the same time). The number of deputies, about 350, are elected according to the size of the population

Section 9: Europe—Spain (cont.)

of their province, but there must be at least two members from each province. Some senators (208) are elected and others (56) are appointed. The Congress makes and approves laws; it is the more powerful of the two houses in the National Assembly. The Senate can try to alter laws but cannot stop their enactment. Although there are many smaller political parties, e.g., the Basque Nationalist Party, the most influential are the Spanish Socialist Workers Party (PSOE) and the United Left (IU) Coalition.

The **judicial** branch at the national level is complex and a bit difficult to comprehend or understand. It is divided into five jurisdictions. A **jurisdiction** is an area of law over which a court may exercise its authority. For example, in the criminal jurisdiction or area, the courts may hear cases involving crimes such as counterfeiting (making fake money) and terrorism. It may not preside over or review a case that deals with civil, military, or other matters. Those cases are reserved for the other courts that have jurisdiction or authority in those areas. The highest court in the land is the Supreme Court or Tribunal Supremo.

What really sets Spain apart from most nations is the way it is organized. It is divided into 17 regional **communities** (think states). Each community is **autonomous** (free to act). These autonomous regional communities have their own governments and a wide range of powers.

Parc Guell in Barcelona, Spain, designed by architect Antonio Gaudi

Each has **provinces** (think counties). The national government allots or gives a great deal of authority and power to the 17 communities. So, Spain is like Switzerland in this regard. It is broken down into a group or federation of 17 communities (and two autonomous cities) that have their own executive, legislative, and judicial branches. This approach to government was approved in the constitution of 1978 and has worked fairly well for the citizens of Spain. Another way to describe Spain is as a nation of 17 independent regions agreeing to be part of a national framework of government. Imagine if all 50 states in America were to be independent yet cooperate with the government in Washington, D.C. For instance, every state could choose its own health care, educational, and welfare programs without consulting with the federal government.

Section 9: Europe—Spain (cont.)

Major Issues:

1. **Gender equality.** Spain has steadily improved access and opportunities for women in government and the workplace. For example, about one-third of the members of Congress are women.

2. **Unevenness.** As you read in the material above, Spain is divided into 17 regions. Each region can decide how it will provide basic care and services, e.g., medical, garbage collection, etc., for its citizens. This means that there is great unevenness in the quality and quantity of care as well as the costs for both. What one region decides about an issue such as water pollution can have a direct effect on other regions. So, unevenness can also mean inequality and result in a lower standard of life for citizens.

3. **Separatist movement.** Related to #2, in 2017, the region of Catalonia voted in a referendum for independence. Many have argued that Catalonia contributes more to the national government than it gets back in benefits. The central government of Spain rejected the referendum and arrested the leaders of the Catalan government, including the president.

What You Should Also Know:

- Bullfighting is viewed as a form of artistic expression in Spain.

- People eat lunch around 2:00 P.M. and dinner between 9:00 and 10:00 P.M.

- Spain is seen as a major shipment point for the international traffic in drugs.

- Illegal immigration, especially from North Africa, continues to be a growing problem.

- Spain suffers from a steady increase in the rate of AIDS.

Name: _____ Date: _____

Section 9: Europe—Spain (cont.)

Directions: Complete the following exercises.

Matching:

____ 1. plurality

____ 2. fascism

____ 3. parliamentary monarchy

____ 4. hereditary

____ 5. autonomous

a. by birth

b. has the most votes

c. government where independent rights are second to the will of the dictator

d. government with a king and executive, legislative, and judicial branches

e. free to act

Fill in the Blank:

6. The _____ of Spain is nominated by the king and approved by the Congress of Deputies.

7. The National Assembly is _____ or has two houses.

8. In the criminal _____, the courts may only hear cases involving crimes.

9. The _____ and autonomous cities of Spain have their own executive, legislative, and judicial branches.

10. Spain has improved access and opportunities for _____ in government and the workplace.

Constructed Response:

11. What are the different parts of the executive branch of the government of Spain?

_____

_____

_____

_____

_____

_____

_____

Section 10: Middle East—Saudi Arabia

Motto: "There is no god other than Allah and Muhammad is his messenger."
<https://www.cia.gov/library/publications/resources/the-world-factbook/geos/sa.html>

Snapshot:

The Kingdom of Saudi Arabia, also known as The Kingdom, is a **monarchy**. The king has the final word on most matters and issues at all levels of government. He rules absolutely and cannot be challenged. He is viewed as both the head of government and its chief of state. There are no political parties or national elections. Local elections are rare and only men can vote. The **legislative** branch is called a Council of Ministers. It is staffed by men chosen by the king. Almost all forms of power—religious, political, financial—rest within the royal family.

Government in a Nutshell:

If you are wondering how this system of government can succeed, keep these facts in mind:

- Politics, government, and religion are merged. The king has authority to make sure that The Kingdom stays true to the values and rules of Islam.

- The Kingdom adheres to the ***Qur'an*** (holy book of Islam) for guidance in running the government and the country. The *Qur'an* is the constitution. The constitution therefore is treated as a holy document that all residents of The Kingdom must obey.

- **Sharia** (Islamic) law is a part of this constitution.

- The **judicial** branch is a system of religious courts. The king has the final say in court cases.

- The legal codes of The Kingdom permit physical punishment for crimes, including such things as flogging, beheading, stoning to death, and cutting off hands and feet.

- The country has borders with Iraq, Jordan, Kuwait, Oman, Qatar, and Yemen.

Shubra Palace in Taif was once used as a summer home by the kings of Saudi Arabia.

- Saudi Arabia is a **welfare state**, which means that the government pays for most services for its citizens, like health care and education.

Section 10: Middle East—Saudi Arabia (cont.)

Under the *Qur'an,* many activities that westerners take for granted are forbidden in The Kingdom, such as:

- Women have few basic civil rights and protections. Sharia law requires all females to submit to the will of men. The views of women do not matter in the government of Saudi Arabia.

- Criticism of the king or government is punishable with a prison sentence without the benefit of a trial.

- Laws are passed through written statements, not by the votes of elected representatives.

- Citizens have no real voice in government.

- Only men can vote, starting at age 21.

In 1992, the Basic Law of Government was introduced. It said that The Kingdom of Saudi Arabia would be ruled by a king. Since then, The Kingdom has changed little of its political system. The government operates with the king at its center. Religious courts review and apply their verdicts to civil cases, using their version of the Holy *Qur'an* as a guide.

The Kingdom is broken into 13 provinces. Each province is run by a relative of the king. Most key jobs in government are held by members of the royal family or persons selected by the king. The crown prince (think vice president) is the next in line to be king upon the death or serious illness of the monarch. In all cases, both the king and all persons must obey the rules of the *Qur'an.* Islamic law is based on the *Qur'an.*

Major Issues:

1. **Population boom.** In the last 30 years, the population of Saudi Arabia jumped from 7 to 28.5 million people. Add to this problem the fact that The Kingdom is faced with a severe water shortage.

2. **Lack of rights for women.** Females have very few rights and freedoms. For example, a woman cannot be seen in public with a man who is not part of her family. Women cannot run for office, run a business, or have real power in The Kingdom.

Section 10: Middle East—Saudi Arabia (cont.)

3. **Bad neighbors.** The Kingdom shares borders with Yemen and Iraq, countries known for their support of terrorism.

What You Should Also Know:

- The Kingdom of Saudi Arabia is an echo from the past. Until the discovery of huge oil fields in the 1930s, it was a bystander in world affairs.

- Oil rules the country. The Kingdom of Saudi Arabia thrives on the income of its oil production. Over 85% of its budget revenues come from oil. Imagine if the United States were to make most of its money from a single source, such as auto production.

- It is a place of contrasts—very little water, huge spreads of deep desert, and massive reserves of oil.

- Men and women may not work together or be seen together at any public events.

- Women were allowed to drive legally for the first time in 2018.

- The Kingdom is the birthplace of Islam.

- A portion of the revenue from oil production is spent on social services such as education, housing, and medical care for its citizens. The bulk of the wealth in The Kingdom, however, goes to the royal family.

It is, in short, a fairly simple system of government. Just keep in mind that the king rules by having the most power placed in his hands.

Name: _____ Date: _____

Section 10: Middle East—Saudi Arabia (cont.)

Directions: Complete the following exercises.

Matching:

____ 1. monarchy   a. The government pays for most services for its citizens
____ 2. *Qur'an*   b. Islamic law
____ 3. welfare state   c. ruled by a king
____ 4. Sharia   d. next in line to be king
____ 5. crown prince   e. holy book of Islam

Fill in the Blank:

6. The king and all persons must obey the rules of the *Qur'an*. The *Qur'an* is the _____ as well as a holy document.

7. Almost all forms of power rest within the _____ family.

8. Criticism of the king or government is punishable with a prison sentence without the benefit of a _____.

9. The views of _____ do not matter in the government of Saudi Arabia.

10. Over 85% of Saudi Arabia's budget revenues come from _____.

Critical Thinking:

11. What are some advantages and disadvantages of having a government ruled by a monarch? Give specific examples to support your answer.

_____

_____

_____

_____

_____

_____

_____

_____

_____

Section 10: Middle East—Turkey

"Peace at Home, Peace in the World"
<https://www.cia.gov/library/publications/resources/the-world-factbook/geos/tu.html>

Snapshot:

Take a look at a world map. This country sits at a key crossroads where the West (Europe) meets the East (Asia). Because of its location, Turkey has been home to many influences, peoples, and cultures that have moved through or settled in that country over the centuries. Study the history of Turkey. You will find a country that has changed "owners" many times. Great empires came and went, rose and fell in Turkey. The basic religion today is Islam. Turkey's population is mostly made up of Sunni Muslims, but the government is fairly independent. If you examine this country closer, you will learn that it has become a very successful nation. Turkey fits nicely in the ranks of modern, developed countries.

The government is **secular**; unlike Saudi Arabia, it has no religious base. It is **centralized** (power resides with the central government in Ankara), and the political system includes such things as a constitution, a **unicameral** (one-house) parliament, and elections every five years in which its citizens can vote for representatives. Turkey is a **republican parliamentary democracy**, somewhat like England's government. This is a more representative type of government compared to Saudi Arabia and other strict governments in the Middle East like Iran and Kuwait.

Government in a Nutshell:

The **executive** branch has two officers. The president is the chief of state in Turkey. That person serves for five years, must be at least 40 years old, and cannot belong to a political party while in office. The president speaks for the nation on official matters but has limited

Ankara, the capital of Turkey

executive power. He is an official spokesperson for the country or state. The parliament elects a person for the office of prime minister. A prime minister is viewed as the head of government. He takes care of the everyday running of the government and is helped by a council of ministers. One part of his job is to organize the government and its many agencies so that things run smoothly. Normally, the prime minister comes from the majority party in the parliament. That is the party with the most elected members.

Section 10: Middle East—Turkey (cont.)

The **legislative** part of the Turkish government is the parliament or Grand National Assembly. It has only one house (unicameral). The citizens vote for their candidates to sit in the parliament for five-year terms. There are several dozen political parties from the 81 provinces (think states) who try to get their candidates elected. Only those parties that get at least 10% of the popular vote can have representatives or delegates in the parliament. The legislature works with the prime minister and government agencies to make and pass laws for the good of the country. The parliament, prime minister, and government agencies (bureaus) help administer the 81 provinces. Overall, the National Assembly performs the following duties:

- Makes and passes laws

- Reviews the national budget (how money will be spent and how much)

- Has the power to declare war

- Supervises the decisions and actions of the prime minister and the council of ministers

In short, the 600 members of the National Assembly are expected to look out for the best interests of the citizens and the entire nation. It acts as a check on the possible abuse of power by the executive branch.

The court or **judicial** system is an independent part of government. It consists of various courts such as the Constitutional Court (reviews laws), a Military Court of Appeals, a Supreme Court of Appeals (Court of Cassation), and others. The Turkish constitution states that no one person or group can prevent the daily operations or decisions of the court system. The judiciary is able to ensure that the spirit and intent of the constitution is protected. The parliament and the executive branch must obey the ruling of the courts. There are different types of courts depending on the type of issue or problem, e.g., children's court, military court, etc.

Major Issues:

1. **Terrorism.** Turkey has been faced with a growing level of violence related to assorted terrorist groups, including Kurdish rebels. Bombings, attacks on tourists, kidnappings, and raids against police continue to plague the country.

2. **Second government.** Turkey has one of the largest armed forces in the region. It is the single strongest institution in

Section 10: Middle East—Turkey (cont.)

the nation. When military leaders feel that the government is moving away from its secular roots (non-religious) or making the wrong decisions, they are willing to seize the reins of power. In a very real sense, the military is a very powerful political group. It can influence the efforts of the executive, legislative, and judicial arms of government.

3. In 2019, after parliamentary and presidential elections, Turkey's government will change to an executive presidential system of government. The president will become both the head of state and the executive head of government. President Recep Tayyip Erdogan is currently exercising these powers after the elections in June 2018 returned him to office.

What You Should Also Know:

- The Trojan Wars happened in western Turkey.

- Istanbul is the only city in the world that is located on two continents.

- There are many ancient underground cities in Turkey that are several hundred years old. Some are very large and buried deep beneath the earth. People would live in them to avoid enemy armies and religious persecution.

- Turkey does not allow trials by jury. All courts are supposed to be open to the public to sit in and observe.

Istanbul

Name: _____ Date: _____

Section 10: Middle East—Turkey (cont.)

Directions: Complete the following exercises.

Matching:

____ 1. centralized
____ 2. secular
____ 3. unicameral
____ 4. prime minister
____ 5. republican parliamentary democracy

a. citizens elect representatives, and the parliament chooses the executive head of government
b. power resides with the central government
c. the head of government
d. non-religious
e. one-house

Fill in the Blank:

6. The prime minister comes from the _____ party in parliament.

7. Only those parties that get at least 10% of the popular vote can have representatives in the _____.

8. The Court of _____ is a supreme court of appeals.

9. The _____ speaks for the nation on official matters but has limited executive power.

10. Turkey sits at the _____ where the West (Europe) meets the East (Asia).

Constructed Response:

11. How does the military influence the government of Turkey? Give specific examples to support your answer.

_____

_____

_____

_____

_____

_____

_____

_____

Section 11: South America—Brazil

"Order and Progress"
<https://www.cia.gov/library/publications/resources/the-world-factbook/geos/br.html>

Snapshot:

Brazil was colonized by Portugal as far back as the early 1500s. The language, values, religion (Catholic), and even the foods and music of Portugal became part of the everyday life of Brazil. Portuguese is the official language, a daily reminder of the nation's close historical tie to its past. Brazil has a long history of turmoil and strife in politics. Rebellions, military dictatorships, and attempts by communists and other groups to control the government continued well into the 1970s. Slowly, Brazil restored civilian rule to the country by introducing a constitution and a government that better represented the interests and will of the diverse people within its boundaries. Brazil is the fifth largest country in the world both in size and population.

Government in a Nutshell:

Brazil is a **federal republic**. It is sometimes called The Brazilian Federation. You may recall that a federation is an arrangement in which a central government disperses certain rights and powers to its states or regions. A federal constitution defines the system of checks and balances within government. It also identifies the types of powers and duties that each of the three branches of government possess. A key point to remember is the layered form of Brazilian government. The constitution gives the federal or central government a great deal of power. Brazil, however, is organized into the following: a federal or central district, 26 states, and over 5,500 municipalities or cities. Power is dispersed among those three groups or levels. There are many similarities between Brazil's government and that of the United States.

The **executive** branch is led by a president who is chief of state, leader of the government, and commander in chief of the military. That person serves for four years, can run for a second term, and appoints a cabinet of advisors to help in running the government. The president of Brazil is a powerful person. Some of his more important duties and powers include the following:

- Authority to declare war against other nations
- Introduce laws to the congress or block proposed laws through a veto
- Uphold and enforce the laws of the constitution
- Make sure the federal government and all of its agencies are running properly

The president of Brazil, by the way, also has an Air Force One jet just like the American president!

Section 11: South America—Brazil (cont.)

The **legislative** branch, located in the city of Brasilia, is known as the National Congress. This lawmaking body tries to represent most of the 27 official political parties of Brazil. The National Congress has two parts or chambers (bicameral). The upper chamber or Senate is made up of 81 senators who serve for eight years. The Senate speaks for the 26 states and the federal district. That works out to three senators for each state and the single district. They look at issues and problems from the point of view of what is good for the state or the majority of people. The lower chamber or House of Deputies has 513 members (deputies) who serve for four years. These legislators tend to look at issues from the vantage point of the needs of the voters who elected them. Both houses seek to write and pass laws that will improve the quality of life for all Brazilians. The laws that are passed cannot be overridden by the states and cities.

The National Congress Building in Brasilia

The **judicial** branch functions solely at the federal and state levels. By far the most important is the Supreme Federal Court, made up of 11 judges. This court interprets and applies the constitution, e.g., announces if a law is illegal or unconstitutional. Other federal courts exist to review laws, treaties, and agreements affecting Brazil. Each of the 26 states has its own judicial system. State courts may not hand down decisions that violate federal rulings or the constitution. All state and federal judges get to keep their jobs for life. This means that the judges cannot be fired if they hand down an unpopular or controversial decision.

Major Issues:

1. **The buck or *real* (Brazillian currency) stops here.** For all of its growth and development, Brazil is a country where the richest 10% get close to 43% of the nation's income. The poor people of Brazil receive less than 1.2% of the wealth. Keep in mind that over 86% of the people in Brazil live in or near cities. Large slums or *favelas* are common, which leads to a second major issue…

2. **Crime.** Brazil is faced with a persistent and widespread crime problem. This is caused by gross poverty, drugs, corrupt police who break laws to make money (*reals*), and the presence of very powerful gangs. Violence, addictive behaviors, and the rise of vigilante groups are also part of the problem of crime in Brazil.

59

Section 11: South America—Brazil (cont.)

3. **Land versus growth.** Brazil has large areas or regions of amazing ecosystems. Half of the country has forests! These regions include the Amazon rain forest, wetlands, pampas, coral reefs, and mangrove swamps, to name but a few. Also, Brazil is home to tens of thousands of plants, animals, and fish species or types. Pressure from cattle ranches, logging, oil industries, and more highways being built through these regions is threatening the habitats and future of the plants, animals, and small native tribes that live there.

What You Should Also Know:

- Everyone who can read and write between the ages of 18 and 70 must vote.

- Because of its size and terrain, Brazil has struggled greatly in trying to improve the quality of life for the bulk of its citizens. Education, health care, housing, and so on remain real challenges for the Brazilian government.

- Of all the countries in the world, Brazil is ranked ninth in the use or consumption of energy.

- Coffee is the national drink in the country.

- Overall **life expectancy** (how long you live) is about 70.5 years for men and 77.7 years for females. On the average, women live about seven years longer than men.

- In 2016, President Dilma Rousseff was impeached and removed from office for mismanaging the budget. She was replaced by Vice President Michel Temer.

The rain forest in Brazil is burned and cut back to make room for farming, industries, and highways.

Name: _____ Date: _____

Section 11: South America—Brazil (cont.)

Directions: Complete the following exercises.

Matching:

____ 1. federal republic

____ 2. *real*

____ 3. *favelas*

____ 4. life expectancy

____ 5. municipalities

a. large slums

b. cities

c. how long you live

d. a central government disperses certain rights and powers to its states or regions

e. Brazillian money

Fill in the Blank:

6. The president is the chief of state, leader of the government, and _____ in chief of the military.

7. _____ is the official language of Brazil.

8. Brazil is organized into a federal district, 26 _____, and 5,500 cities.

9. The National Congress has an upper house or _____ and a lower house or House of _____.

10. All state and federal _____ get to keep their jobs for life.

Constructed Response:

11. What are some examples of poverty and its effects in Brazil?

_____

_____

_____

_____

_____

_____

_____

_____

_____

_____

Section 11: South America—Peru

"Steady and Happy for the Union"
<https://www.cia.gov/library/publications/resources/the-world-factbook/geos/pe.html>

Snapshot:

The histories of Spain and Peru are linked together. In the early 1500s, Spanish warriors or **conquistadors** arrived in Peru. Under the leadership of Francisco Pizarro, this small band was able to overthrow the mighty Inca empire. Spain had sent these soldiers to conquer and plunder (steal) the gold and silver of the native empire located high in the Andes Mountains. Settlers followed, and the country of Peru was turned into a colony of Spain. The Inca and other native tribes were used as slaves in the mines and fields. The country was organized at first with a simple system of government. It was not until 1821 that Peru achieved its independence. Yet, hundreds of years later, we still see proof of Spanish influence on the basic system of government used in Peru.

Government in a Nutshell:

Peru is listed as a **constitutional republic**. It continues to develop into a nation that promotes human rights and a healthy economy. The reality is, however, that Peru's political history is one of strife and problems. Since 1824, the country has been constantly involved in disputes, wars, and overthrows of its governments. The overthrows were led either by the military or the elite—the richest, most powerful families in the country. Add to that mix of events the fact that during the 1980s, the government was waging a brutal war against radical groups such as the Shining Path.

The country has been slowly trying to restore democracy and freedom into its political process. This has been difficult. Former President Fujimori was sentenced to 25 years in prison for human rights crimes. Previous administrations were often figureheads for the military. They acted on behalf of the military, not the citizens of Peru. Since 2006, things have improved. There appears to be reason to hope for a freer, less corrupt government.

The **executive** branch is led by a president. The president can only serve for five years and must be at least 35 years of age. He is elected by a direct popular vote. There are two vice presidents, but neither has any real authority or functions. They serve as back-ups in case the president dies or cannot fulfill his duties. It is the president who is both chief of state and head of the Peruvian government. A council of ministers (think cabinet) is chosen by the president and approved by the congress. Both the president and congress can introduce laws to be enacted or put into force. This means that the president has executive and legislative powers to run the country, a very unique situation. Plus, the president can block a law from being enacted.

Section 11: South America—Peru (cont.)

The **legislative** arm of the government is referred to as the Congress of the Republic of Peru (or just Congress). One hundred thirty people (at least 25 years of age) are elected for five-year terms to preside in the one-house congress. The basic duties of the congress are:

- Draft and pass laws

- Ratify treaties

- Approve government loans and the government budget

- Represent the interests of their voters

Colca Canyon in the Andes Mountains

There are 25 **regions** (think states) and the province of Lima. The regions (except Lima) are further divided into **provinces**. The regions have their own governments in which they can pass local laws. The provinces are broken into **districts**. Roughly 30 political parties operate at the local and national level. It is obviously very difficult for any single party to be dominant or the most powerful in the Congress. What happens is that the different parties form groups or **coalitions** in order to get things done in the Congress and in local politics.

The **judicial** branch is made up of four levels:

1. Supreme Court of the Republic: It has authority over all of Peru in terms of legal matters. This includes crimes, civil cases, e.g. suing someone, and constitutional issues (think national).

2. Superior Courts: These courts listen to cases such as labor, family, and criminal matters within the 25 regions (states).

3. Courts of First Instance: Trial courts found in the provinces (counties)

4. Courts of Peace: A nice term for courts that deal only with cases inside a district (cities)

It is easy to get these court levels confused. Try to remember them on the basis of highest to lowest, with the Supreme Court at the top dealing only with national cases and the Courts of Peace at the bottom. In a sense, the local cases start at the bottom, and the more important ones work their way to the top.

Section 11: South America—Peru (cont.)

Major Issues:

Peru has a history of political upsets, e.g., military rule, democracy, rule by a few rich people, etc. Its single major issue is really several issues all linked together by one common theme—people.

- **Not enough government help.** Peru is like Brazil in several ways. One of these is the fact that too many people live in utter poverty while too few people gather and keep the wealth. The results are very unpleasant, even deadly. For much of the population, good-paying jobs are scarce. Basic health care, good sanitation, drinkable water, and healthy diets are absent. The lack of a retirement system and affordable (cheap) housing has driven citizens into slums or shantytowns. The final outcome is predictable: people do not expect either a healthy or successful life. Without enough support from its government, the gap in services and income between Peru's haves (rich) and the have nots (poor) will keep expanding.

What You Should Also Know:

- Spanish remains the basic language of common use.

- Peru is very rich in mineral resources. It is a top-ranked producer of silver (#1), zinc (#2), copper, tin, lead, and gold.

- Peru is about the same size as Alaska, with a population of 31 million.

- Economic conditions are getting better in Peru. From a recent high of 50%, now about 20 percent of Peruvians live in poverty. Per capita GDP is $12,480 a year. About 3.8 percent of Peruvians live on less than $1.90 a day.

- Earthquakes are common in Peru.

- There are almost 4,000 native varieties of Peruvian potatoes.

Name: _____ Date: _____

Section 11: South America—Peru (cont.)

Directions: Complete the following exercises.

Matching:

____ 1. coalitions

____ 2. conquistadores

____ 3. constitutional republic

____ 4. region

____ 5. council of ministers

a. state

b. groups formed to get things done in politics

c. cabinet

d. government whose powers are limited by a formal constitution and whose leaders are elected

e. Spanish warriors

Fill in the Blank:

6. After the Inca empire was overthrown, Peru became a colony of _____.

7. The president of Peru is elected by a direct _____ vote.

8. Both the _____ and _____ can introduce laws to be enacted.

9. The Supreme Court deals only with _____ cases, and the Courts of Peace deal only with cases inside a _____ or city.

10. About _____ percent of Peruvians live in poverty.

Constructed Response:

11. List at least three different types of government that have existed in Peru.

_____

_____

_____

_____

_____

_____

_____

_____

_____

Section 12: The United Nations

(http://www.un.org/en/.index.html)

There is no other organization like the United Nations or UN. No other agency has erected a huge statue of a pistol with its barrel bent back. That statue is a symbol for a time when the world will no longer need to fight to settle its problems. No other group in the world is made up of 193 nations who come together to do the following:

- **To try to promote and keep world peace.**

- **To serve as a neutral ground for nations to resolve their problems.**

- **To protect peoples of the world who cannot defend themselves from war, bad governments, and disasters.**

- **To wipe out diseases, poverty, and abuses of human rights.**

- **To serve as a symbol of hope in a world torn by human conflicts and environmental problems that affect us all.**

The United Nations began in 1945. Almost every nation has an office and group of delegates at the UN headquarters in New York. It is very important that all nations have a place where they can debate and hopefully resolve or settle issues. The group in which all members sit and discuss is known as the General Assembly. A second group—the Security Council—is smaller, with only 15 delegates. Five of these members are permanent. These are France, Russia, United Kingdom, United States, and China. Another important group within the UN is the International Court of Justice (ICJ). It is based in The Hague, Netherlands. In a sense, the ICJ is the court of the United Nations. It hears cases involving disputes between nations such as:

- International crimes such as piracy, genocide, and the use of illegal weapons against other nations, e.g., chemical gases.
- Arguments about rights and duties of nations, e.g., overfishing the ocean sea beds, use of atomic weapons in outer space.

The United Nations is, in a nutshell, an organization aimed at keeping world peace and protecting human rights. Sometimes, when the need is clear, the UN will send a military peacekeeping force or emergency supplies to nations under great stress. The UN has a very modest track record of success in achieving its goals. Any nation that wants to do so may ignore the decisions of the United Nations and do as it pleases. The UN has no authority or power to make a nation "behave." It can pass resolutions that nations may agree to, and it may issue warnings and even cut off trade or aid to a nation, BUT no country must be a member of the UN or obey its orders.

Section 13: International Law

International law is all about the ideals and guidelines that nations use when dealing with one another. It includes specific laws, treaties, customs, and agreements among nations. The topics are things that could directly affect nations, such as deep-sea mining of the ocean bed and global warming. There is no single set of international laws written down in a book that every country agrees to obey. The idea of international law is different from a nation's own laws. No country has to obey any international law. There is no international court or police agency that can force obedience. However, any nation that chooses to ignore the laws of nations does so at great risk. Other nations may retaliate or respond in harmful ways:

- Refuse to sign treaties with the rogue country
- Decide not to trade with that country
- Refuse to help the country when they require help with an issue, e.g., terrorism
- Send military forces into the country

The idea is that nations are better off when they cooperate with one another for the good of the planet and their citizens. For instance, it is a good thing to allow medical teams to enter war-torn countries and help the injured. An agreement is needed for that to happen. It is also a good thing for nations to agree (via a treaty) not to empty the world's sea beds of fish. You can see that international law is very important in the role of relationships among nations. It sets out areas of concern and cooperation for nations. For example, if a dispute pops up between Brazil and Peru about the proper use of the Amazon rain forests, international law may offer some guidelines on how it can be resolved.

The Peace Palace in The Hague, Netherlands, where the International Court of Justice sits

Just as nations, states, and provinces have laws and regulations to run their countries, the nations of the world need their own set of arrangements. Without these treaties (agreements), general laws, and procedures for dealing with each other, nations would be unable to peacefully or successfully settle most disputes or arguments. For instance, there are rules such as the Geneva Conventions about how to treat the victims of war.

The key word in this section is **agreement**. Governments of the world agree (most of the time) to abide by a set of general laws and treaties as they interact with each other on a wide range of topics and disputes. As you will discover in the treaty activity found on page 73, that is sometimes hard to do.

Section 14: The State of World Governments

You have looked at 13 different governments from around the world. Each country is unique in some ways from the others. It would be useful in this closing section to make some general observations about international governments and political processes. These comments are based on a number of items that we have discussed in the previous sections, such as political parties, economy, social issues, and so on. Also, this is an excellent segue or lead-in to the challenge activities. So, let us consider these closing remarks as preparation or a refresher for the fun activities to follow.

Closing Facts About World Governments

- **Fact:** There is no such thing as a perfect world government. A country is made up of many diverse interests and needs. Its people do not come in one flavor, so to speak, nor do they all agree on how or what they want at any given time. You have read about 13 types of governments and political systems. All are built and maintained by people, and people make mistakes or act in ways that do not promote the good of all. For instance, what is fair in one culture may seem silly or wrong in another. The governments of Sweden, Norway, Finland, and Denmark believe that many social services (retirement, health care, etc.) must be provided to everyone by applying a high tax on wages. Other governments, like Germany and India, believe that people should not be so heavily taxed and that a strong job market will help provide good social services.

- **Fact:** The world is a dangerous place, no matter what type of government is in power. Crime, contagious diseases, wars, gangs, pollution, infant mortality (babies that do not live long), religious fanatics, natural disasters (typhoons, earthquakes, volcanic eruptions), bad highways (yes, tens of thousands of people die on highways around the world), and other hazards are common events throughout the world.

- **Fact:** The most successful governments in the world are those that invite participation from all citizens. This takes the forms of open and fair elections, political parties that represent the concerns of the voters, a constitution and set of laws that identify the rights and duties of all citizens, and a general feeling of support by voters for the basic authority and right of government to rule and uphold the constitution and laws.

Voting in Afghanistan

Section 14: The State of World Governments (cont.)

- **Fact:** To really understand a government, you must study these things:

  ◆ History of the country
  ◆ Culture and norms of the citizens
  ◆ Identity of the nation; what beliefs do the citizens and government prize the most? Some countries such as the United States, South Korea, and Singapore value equality, opportunity (hard work = success), and individual rights. Other countries support or identify with the concept of group rights over those of the individual. Such nations include Japan, China, and Cuba.
  ◆ Economic power of the country. What are the sources of wealth, and how is it spread across the population?

What you have learned with this book is that the governments of the world come in different flavors and forms, some very good (United States, France, Argentina, etc.) while others (Sudan, Haiti, Myanmar, etc.) are either struggling to survive or just downright awful. You may recall that at the start of this book we challenged you to go further and become a student of world affairs. In doing so, you will begin to appreciate how often some event that occurs in one nation can affect other nations.

For example, an increase in the number of autos bought in China in the next five years means the demand for gasoline will increase sharply. This means the cost per gallon of gas will go up around the world, and people in other countries will complain that more of their income or wages are spent on gasoline. Let's keep going with this situation. The governments of oil-producing countries, like Iraq, Venezuela, and Saudi Arabia, will have to decide if they want to raise their production levels (make more oil available to meet the new demand for gas in China). If not, some countries may end up with gasoline shortages. Their economies will weaken. The citizens will blame, among others, the politicians and government.

You get the idea. What happens in another country can cause a chain reaction of events that affects much of the world. It may affect the quality of living, the economy, upset the political process (riots, strikes, civil wars, etc.), and even lead to the overthrow of governments.

In closing, therefore, keep in mind that the world is a fairly small place. In one day's travel, you can fly to any of the countries of the world. You can transport yourself to a very different government (Russia), culture (Egypt), landscape (Amazon River), and way of life (New Zealand). You will need a passport, some money, and a desire to discover the world. You might think of it as a grand adventure with you as the master explorer. Bon voyage!

Name: _____   Date: _____

The Big Wrap Up!

Directions: We have put together a final round of questions that cover many of the high points of the book. This is your final challenge. When you are done answering the questions, refer back to the section(s) and see how you did. Thanks for using this book. We hope it has been an eye-opening journey to other governments and places in the world.

1. A document that you will need to travel to other countries is called a _____. (Section 1)

2. When one country conquers and takes over another country, it is known as _____. (Section 2).

3. _____ is when nations try to settle their problems and differences without using force. (Section 2)

4. What is infrastructure, and why is it important to a country? (Section 2)

    _____

    _____

    _____

5. Name two pieces or parts of a nation, e.g., set of laws. (Section 3)

    • _____

    • _____

6. What is a difference between a democracy and a dictatorship? (Section 4)

    _____

    _____

    _____

7. The three parts of a government are known as the _____, _____, and _____ branches. (Section 5)

8. Name one goal of the United Nations. (Section 12) _____

    _____

9. _____ law is all about the rules and guidelines nations use when dealing with one another. (Section 13)

10. To really understand another government, what are some of the things you should study? (Section 14) _____

    _____

    _____

Constitutions of the World: Challenge Activity

Throughout the book, we have talked about constitutions. A **constitution** is a document that has values, ideas, and an order or structure for a government. It is a vital document that binds a nation and its people together. Words have power. Nowhere is this more true than in the words of a nation's constitution. The constitution of a government lays out the duties and rights of all citizens. So, it does matter very much what words are found within a constitution. This challenge is meant to get you acquainted with the constitutions of other countries.

Directions:

1. Use the following website:

    Constitute Project

    https://www.constituteproject.org

2. Select any two countries from the list of nations.

3. Click on the constitutions (English versions) of the two nations.

4. On the following page, write down two important ideas that are different between the constitutions of the two countries.

5. Fill in the Compare & Contrast Chart on page 74 with information about the two important ideas in the constitutions of the two countries.

Name: _____ Date: _____

Constitutions of the World: Challenge Activity (cont.)

Nations:

Country #1: _____

Ideas:

   1. _____

      _____

      _____

      _____

   2. _____

      _____

      _____

      _____

Country #2: _____

Ideas:

   1. _____

      _____

      _____

      _____

   2. _____

      _____

      _____

Exercise in Treaties

A **treaty** is an agreement between two or more nations to start or stop doing something. For example, several nations may agree to help build a hydroelectric plant and share the electricity that it generates. A treaty is also something that is mutual; each nation understands that it must honor its promise to do or not do something. Israel and Palestine have long been arguing and fighting over land that both sides believe is not to be shared with the other. No treaty has yet been forged and honored by both sides. Eventually one or both nations violate or break an agreement not to interfere with the rights of the other to exist. Both sides (governments) think they are absolutely right.

Directions: In this exercise, you will be asked to form into small groups (nations). The topic is this:

"A treaty is needed for the sharing of the ocean's resources."

Your group must draft an agreement that states how the ocean's resources—fish, minerals, sea beds, clean waters—are to be used by the nations of the world. This will take some time to sort out the tougher issues, such as overfishing by some nations. See what sorts of things matter the most to you in terms of safeguarding the oceans of the world.

It may be helpful to use the Compare & Contrast Chart on page 74 to highlight some of the major differences and similarities between two of the countries involved in the negotiations.

Put your statement or agreement into general terms or language. Discuss it with other groups. Add or subtract other ideas and terms. The goal is to create a successful treaty that will last for generations. Share the final version(s) of what your group wants in the treaty with the class, and see what the other groups (nations) agree upon.

Name: _____ Date: _____

Compare & Contrast Chart

Directions: Use the chart below to compare and contrast two different nations or two types of governments.

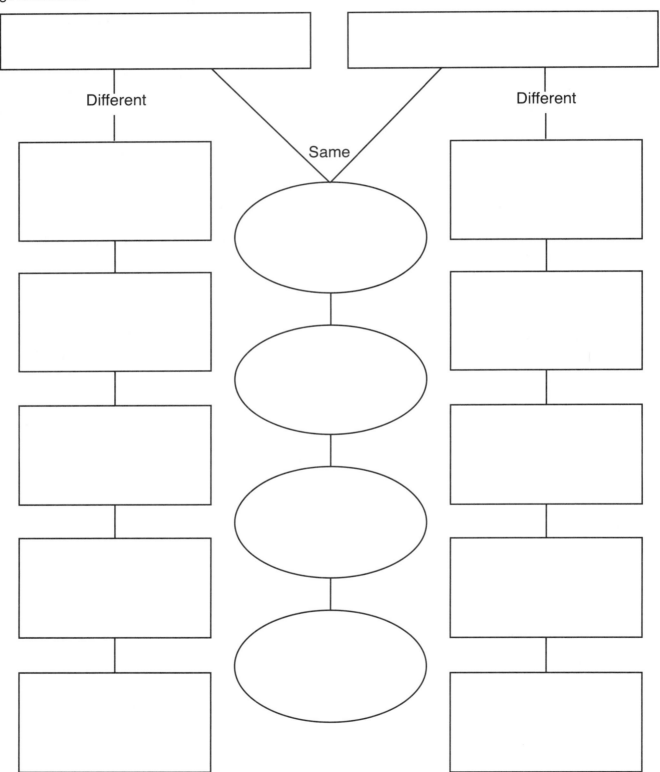

Reference Sources

Websites

All About Turkey
Istanbul
www.allaboutturkey.com/istanbul.htm

The Trojan Wars
www.allaboutturkey.com/troy.htm

Altapedia Online
www.atlapedia.com

CIA: The World Factbook Online
https://www.cia.gov/library/publications/
resources/the-world-factbook/index.html

Global Security.org
www.globalsecurity.org

GlobaLex: New York Univerisity Law
Global Law Center
www.nyulawglobal.org/Globalex/

Library of Congress: Guide to Law Online:
Nations
www.loc.gov/law/help/guide/nations.php

Nation Master
www.nationmaster.com

The Nations Online Project
www.nationsonline.org

The United Nations
www.un.org/en/index.html

Wikipedia
www.wikipedia.com

Worldwide Governments on the WWW
www.gksoft.com/govt

Books

The World Factbook 2018. Washington, D.C.: Central Intelligence Agency. 2018.

Exploring World Governments (series). Edina, MN: Essential Publishing. 2010–11.

Giesecke, Ernestine. *Governments Around the World*. Mankato, MN: Heinemann-Raintree. 2010.

The World Almanac and Book of Facts, 2018. New York: The World Almanac®. 2017.

Note: In addition to the above sources, the authors referred to numerous documents (monographs, agency reports, etc.) to assist in the review and description of each nation and their respective governments. These documents (foreign and American) cover a period from 2005 to 2018. There are mountains of free documents on all sorts of international topics for students. Many of the items are available on the Internet. The above list, however, is a very good launching point for your studies. We recommend that you pick a topic, e.g., the use of children as soldiers, and refer to one of the references such as the United Nations. You will be surprised at what you find.

Answer Keys

Section 2: Glossary—Key Terms of World Politics, Crossword Puzzle (p. 8)

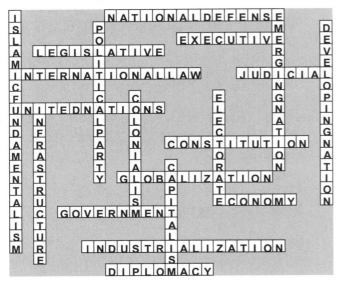

Section 4: Types of World Governments, Word Search Puzzle (p. 14)

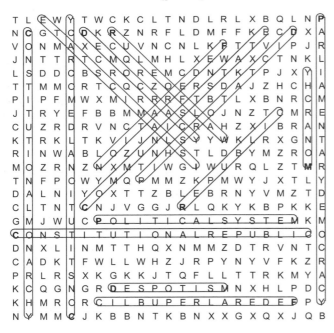

Section 5: United States of America (p. 19)
1. c   2. d   3. a   4. e
5. b
6. Constitution   7. federal, state, local
8. executive, legislative, judicial

9. backlash   10. Supreme Court
11. No. The Supreme Court reviews laws and can declare them unconstitutional. The executive branch may not cooperate with the legislature if it passes laws the executive doesn't like.

Section 6: Africa—Mauritius (p. 22)
1. d   2. c   3. e   4. a
5. b
6. environment
7. president, prime minister
8. French, English   9. police
10. five
11. Possible answers include: It has regular elections. The goal of the government is to promote democratic values like free speech, human rights, literacy, and a vigorous economy. They are trying to safeguard the environment. Trade, agriculture, tourism, and manufacturing make the nation an economic success.

Section 6: Africa—South Africa (p. 26)
1. d   2. e   3. b   4. a
5. c
6. legislative   7. apartheid
8. Bloemfontein
9. National Assembly   10. Pretoria
11. Possible answers include: They could not vote or hold office. They needed a government pass to work. They had no civil rights. They received few services. There was complete separation of public facilities.

Section 7: Asia—China (p. 31)
1. e   2. a   3. d   4. b
5. c
6. communism   7. jobs, competing
8. Communist Party, China
9. People's Liberation
10. Congress

11. Answer will vary. Possible answers include: China has achieved great success in developing its economy and is now the second largest economy in the world. Its military is also very strong. However, its citizens have no basic freedoms, such as freedom of speech. The government does not allow dissent and uses torture to control its people.

Section 7: Asia—Thailand (p. 35)
1. d   2. c   3. e   4. a
5. b
6. figurehead   7. no confidence
8. bills   9. Juries
10. Laos, Myanmar
11. Possible answers include: Prime ministers have been removed or resigned since 2008. The military overthrew the government in 2006. Not until 2001 was it able to complete a full term. Another coup occurred in 2014, and a general is the interim prime minister. Since 1932, the constitution has changed 20 times. They have had a variety of governmental forms.

Section 8: Central America and Caribbean Basin—Costa Rica (p. 38)
1. d   2. a   3. e   4. b
5. c
6. Central America   7. Spanish
8. vice presidents   9. terms
10. infrastructure
11. Possible answers include: They come into the country and use resources and social services, such as medical care, welfare, and schooling. The government doesn't get paid for these services, since illegal immigrants usually don't pay taxes and refugees have no money.

Section 8: Central America and Caribbean Basin—Honduras (p. 41)
1. b   2. d   3. a   4. e
5. c
6. whims   7. president
8. Mayan   9. Hurricane Mitch
10. gangs
11. Possible answers include: It is very poor, badly managed, kept going through military force, and relies on foreign aid from the United States.

Section 9: Europe—Switzerland (p. 45)
1. b   2. c   3. e   4. a
5. d
6. banking   7. Rural flight
8. parliament   9. wealth
10. cantons
11. Answers will vary. It can be considered good because the parliament is elected by the people. However, there is no real separation between the legislative and executive branches, since the people do not get to elect the executive.

Section 9: Europe—Spain (p. 49)
1. b   2. c   3. d   4. a
5. e
6. president   7. bicameral
8. jurisdiction   9. communities
10. women
11. The executive branch is made up of a hereditary king, a president appointed by the king and approved by the Congress of Deputies, a Council of Ministers, and a Council of State.

Section 10: Middle East—Saudi Arabia (p. 53)

1. c   2. e   3. a   4. b
5. d
6. constitution   7. royal
8. trial   9. women
10. oil
11. Possible answers include:
    Advantages: It is a simple form of government. There is no need for lots of government agencies and offices. It is easier for the king to get things done. Disadvantages: The people have little input in the government. They never know what kind of king they'll get. The next in line just inherits the job. Wealth and power are all in one family. Citizens only have the rights the king gives them.

Section 10: Middle East—Turkey (p. 57)

1. b   2. d   3. e   4. c
5. a
6. majority   7. parliament
8. Cassation   9. president
10. crossroads
11. Possible answers include: It is one of the largest armed forces in the area, so it has a lot of power. Military leaders may seize power if they feel the government is moving away from its secular roots or making the wrong decisions.

Section 11: South America—Brazil (p. 61)

1. d   2. e   3. a   4. c
5. b
6. commander   7. Portuguese
8. states   9. Senate, Deputies
10. judges
11. Possible answers include: The poor people receive less than 1.2% of the wealth. Most people live in cities where large slums are common. Crime is widespread. Police break laws to make money. Gangs take advantage of the situation. The government struggles to provide education, health care, and housing to its citizens.

Section 11: South America—Peru (p. 65)

1. b   2. e   3. d   4. a
5. c
6. Spain   7. popular
8. president, congress
9. national, district
10. 20
11. Peru has been a colony of Spain, ruled by the military, ruled by the elite, and is currently a constitutional republic.

The Big Wrap Up! (p. 70)

1. passport
2. colonialism
3. Diplomacy
4. Infrastructure is all the internal items that are needed to keep a country running. It includes highways, the postal service, water supply, power grids and plants, telecommunications, buildings, etc. Not much can get accomplished without a well-run infrastructure.
5. Answers will vary. Accept any two from the nation list in Section 3.
6. Answers will vary. Possible answers include: In a democracy, the majority rules. In a dictatorship, one person has complete authority over a nation. A democracy promotes a wide range of liberties and freedoms. Individual rights are not important in a dictatorship.
7. executive, legislative, and judicial
8. Answers will vary. Accept goals listed in Section 12.
9. International
10. You must study the history of the country, the culture and norms of the citizens, the identify of the nation, and the economic power of the country.